STUDY WORKBOOK FOR ISBN 978-1933039572

Mortgage Lending Loan Officer Training

Library of Congress -in-Publication Data
October 2012

Mortgage Lending – Loan Officer Study Workbook for ISBN 978-1933039626

Printed in the United States of America

10 9 8 7 6 5 4 3 2 1

The enclosed material is designed for educational purposes only. Each State may have different certification and specific guidelines. Please refer to your State for additional and future information. The information contained herein is considered correct at the time of creation but laws and regulations are updated frequently and the reader assumes the responsibility for confirming current regulations and applicable data. The publisher and author make no warranty as to the success of the individuals using the training material contained herein. The publisher and author make no warranty as to any action taken by any individual completing this program. The reader is responsible for the appropriate use of the materials and information provided. This publication is designed to provide accurate and authoritative information concerning the subject matter. All material is sold with the understanding that neither the author nor the publisher guarantees the actions of any individual making use of the inclusions. Neither the author nor the publisher is rendering a legal opinion, accounting recommendation or other professional service. If legal advice or other expert assistance is desired, the services of a legal professional or other individual should be sought. The applicable federally released forms, disclosures and notices are generated from public domain. Copyright law does apply to all intellectual materials and all rights under said law are reserved b y the copyright owner.

Coursework is available at special quantity discounts to use as premiums and sales promotions within corporate or private training programs. To obtain information or inquire about availability please write to Director, PO Box 1, Hollidaysburg, PA 16648.

STUDY WORKBOOK FOR ISBN 978-1933039626

Mortgage Lending Loan Officer Training

Flashcard Set

The flashcard set is designed to assist you in testing you retention of the materials. You should complete the coursework and then use a file card to cover the second row that contains the answers to each question. Review the questions and then check your answers.

When you feel you are ready for enhanced testing, complete the self-test segments of the workbook. Completing the self-tests without reference to the written text is the best method of assessing your knowledge base. If you are unable to answer a particular question, you should review the applicable chapter in its entirety.

What are the two classifications within the mortgage market?

- Banks and Brokerages
- Investing Pools and Individuals
- Primary Market and Secondary Market
- Banks and Savings Institutions

The two classifications within the mortgage market are the primary and the secondary mortgage market.

What is the purpose of a mortgage broker?

A Mortgage Broker acts as a liaison between the borrowers seeking mortgage funds and multiple funding sources.

What are the three most common employment opportunities for a loan Officer?

- Government, Conventional, Other
- A Paper, B/C Paper, Nonconforming
- Prime, Sub-Prime, Conventional
- Bank, Brokerage, E Commute

The three most common employment opportunities for a loan Officer are Bank, Brokerage, and E-Commuting.

What is a Loan Origination?

The process by which a mortgage lender obtains a mortgage secured by real property. An origination fee is charged by the lender to process all forms involved in obtaining a mortgage.

Which is not a common entity within the primary mortgage market?

- Mortgage Brokerage Office
- Mutual Savings Bank
- Credit Union
- Insurance Company

An Insurance Company is not a common entity within the primary mortgage market.

What is Freddie Mac?

Nickname for Federal Home Loan Mortgage Corp A financial corporation chartered by the federal government to buy pools of mortgages from lenders and sell securities backed by these mortgages.

What is an investing pool?

An Investing Pool is a group of smaller investors seeking a low risk, long term investment and having capital available to purchase packaged loan products.

What is Ginnie Mae?

Nickname for the Government National Mortgage Association

What is HUD?

- Homeowners Underwriting Department
- Department of Housing in Urban Developments
- Department of Housing and Urban Development
- None of the Above

HUD
Department of Housing and Urban Development

What is the purpose of the laws that govern the ethics and disclosures with which you handle loan processes?

The laws and acts governing ethics and disclosure practices are in place to protect the interest of the public and make the obtainment of housing and home mortgage funds a fair practice for all applicants.

What is PMI?

- Personal Mortgage Insurance
- Private Mortgage Insurance
- Public Mortgage Insurance
- Premium Mortgage Insurance

PMI
Private Mortgage Insurance

What is the Fair Credit Reporting Act ?

A consumer protection law that regulates the disclosure of consumer credit reports by credit reporting agencies and establishes procedures for correcting mistakes on a person's credit record.

What act assists in the prevention of discrimination against applicants?

- HMDA and ECOA
- ECOA and Fair Housing
- Fair Housing and RESPA
- RESPA and HMDA

ECOA and Fair Housing Acts assist in the prevention of discrimination against applicants.

What items are illegal for use in evaluating applicant's qualifications?

- Race, color, religion, sex, national origin, marital status, age, source of income, handicap, and familial status
- Credit, employment, mortgage or rental history, and property value
- Race, color, religion, Credit, employment, mortgage or rental history, and property value
- None of the Above

Race, color, religion, sex, national origin, marital status, age, source of income, handicap, and familial status are illegal for use in evaluating applicant's qualifications.

When must a right to cancel be provided?

- At the settlement meeting
- When a borrower refinances their primary residence
- When a borrower obtains a loan against their primary residence
- When a borrower refinances any property

A notice of the borrower's right to cancel must be provided in relationship to any credit transaction that involves a security interest in a borrower's primary residence.

Why have ethics and disclosure laws been created?

* To provide the lender with a series of practical directions
* To protect the interest of the public
* To make the obtainment of mortgage funds a fair practice
* All of the above

Ethics and disclosure laws been created to provide the lender with a series of practical directions, to protect the interest of the public, and to make the obtainment of mortgage funds a fair practice.

The Loan Officer must:

• Educate the consumer
• Act in an ethical manner
• Incorporate the required practices into their daily workload
• All of the above

The Loan Officer must educate the consumer, act in an ethical manner, and incorporate fair practices into their daily workload.

Many states have created educational and licensure requirements for lending professionals.

True
False

It is true that many states have created educational and licensure requirements for lending professionals.

In 1937, what agency was created to enable more Americans to become homeowners?

- Federal Housing Acceptance
- Federal Homeowners Association
- Federal Housing Administration
- Federal Housing Authority

In 1937, the Federal Housing Administration was created to enable more Americans to become homeowners.

HMDA requires the reporting of

- Pipeline Reports
- Loan Origination Referral Data
- Public Loan Data
- None of the Above

HMDA requires the reporting of Public Loan Data

Information for the HMDA reports should be gathered:

 At the closing table
At the time of pre-qualification
At the initial application
During post-close processes

Information for the HMDA reports should be gathered at the initial application.

.

HUD is a direct lender.

• True
• False

HUD is a NOT a direct lender of mortgage funds.

The automatic insurance premium
cancellation requires that the principal
balance of the loan fall below:

- 85%
- 82%
- 80%
- 78%

The automatic insurance premium
cancellation requires that the principal
balance of the loan fall below 78%.

Fair housing laws are designed to prevent

Discrimination in a credit related
transaction

Discrimination in the setting of application
appointments

Too many underprivileged loan
disbursements

None of the above

Fair housing laws are designed to
prevent discrimination in a credit
related transaction.

ECOA is

- Equal Credit Origination Act
- Every Credit Opportunity Agenda
- Equal Credit Opportunity Act
- None of the Above

ECOA
Equal Credit Opportunity Act

ECOA addresses:

- Discriminatory Actions
- Predatory Lending Tactics
- Required Action Disclosures
- All of the Above

ECOA addresses Discriminatory Actions, Predatory Lending Tactics, and Required Disclosures

RESPA

- Helps consumers shop for settlement services
- Eliminates referral fees
- Requires specific borrower disclosures
- All of the above

RESPA helps consumers shop for settlement services, eliminates referral fees, and requires specific borrower disclosures

---

The borrower has the right to cancel any credit transaction involving their home within 3 days of the funding of the transaction.

- True
- False

TRUE - The borrower has the right to cancel any credit transaction involving their home within 3 days of the funding of the transaction.

What are Closing Costs?

Expenses incurred by buyers and sellers in transferring ownership of a property. Closing costs normally include an origination fee, an attorney's fee, taxes, escrow payments, and charges for title insurance. Lenders or Real Estate Agents provide estimates of closing costs to prospective homebuyers.

You will request a credit authorization before pulling borrower credit.

- True
- False

TRUE - You must request a credit authorization before pulling borrower credit.

What is the score range you can expect to see on a credit report?

- 450-850
- 500-700
- 620-850
- 620-750

You can expect to see a credit score range of 450-850 on a credit report.

What credit bureau you will you use for most borrowers?

Beacon at Equifax
Empirica at Transunion
TRW/Fair Isaac at TRW

are the three credit reporting agencies. The one that is considered most applicable to the region will be used for the loan program.

Fair, Isaac credit bureau scores do NOT use what as predictive characteristics:

- Race, color, religion, national origin, sex, marital status
- Age, occupation, length of time at present housing
- Any information not contained within the credit file
- Any of the Above

Fair, Isaac credit bureau scores use only that information that is contained within the credit file.

How can you gain information to understand why a credit report scored the way it did?

- From the pre-qualification questionnaire
- Through your application meeting with the borrower
- By reviewing the score factor reason codes
- Through the issuance of a credit supplement

The score factor reason codes will provide the top reasons why a credit report scored the way it did.

Credit Reports are:

A great way to see how many things people buy

A way to get to know a borrower's likes and dislikes

An overview of a person's entire history of spending and payment

None of the above

Credit Reports are an overview of a person's entire history of spending and payment.

The ability to borrow more money is affected by

- How much debt potential a borrower currently carries
- How many things a borrower has in his house
- How a borrower treats you and your company
- All of the above

The ability to borrow more money is affected by how much debt potential a borrower currently carries and their history of making payments on that debt.

A bankruptcy can remain on a credit report for

- 3 years
- 7 years
- 10 years
- Life

A bankruptcy can remain on a credit report for up to 10 years.

Credit reports are an overview of a person's history of spending and payment habits.

- True
- False

True - Credit reports are an overview of a person's history of spending and payment habits.

Accounts to medical services that a borrower has failed to pay as agreed are

- Often treated differently
- Never a concern
- An underwriting condition
- Always to be paid in full

Accounts to medical services that a borrower has failed to pay as agreed are often treated differently than other collection accounts.

Repeatedly requesting a borrower's credit report may

- Adversely effect the credit score
- Show the borrower's can obtain further credit
- Cause an underwriting condition
- All of the above

Repeatedly requesting a borrower's credit report may adversely effect the credit score and cause an underwriting condition requiring an explanation that the repeated inquiries were a result of the mortgage shopping process.

A late payment is any payment paid past the due date even when within the grace period

True
False

False - A late payment is any payment paid past the grace period.

What is your primary concern when reviewing a borrower's credit report?

- Any mortgage payments showing on the report
- The last 18 months of the credit history
- Any action that created a negative or derogatory entry on the report
- All of the Above

When you review the credit report, your primary concern is any negative or derogatory entry on the report.

Credit bureau scores are based upon

every action taken by a borrower with regard to debt

the data contained within the credit bureau

all information contained within the loan application

none of the above

Credit bureau scores are only based on the items found within the credit file.

A credit bureau score will rank order potential borrowers based upon the number of good loans to bad loans.

- True
- False

TRUE - A credit bureau score will rank order potential borrowers based upon the number of good loans to bad loans.

What monthly payment amount will you enter for a revolving liability that currently has no balance?

- $0.00
- $15.00
- $25.00
- 2% of the credit line available

It is common practice to factor a $15.00 monthly payment amount for a revolving liability that currently has no balance.

Gross Income is

Income after taxes
Income before taxes
Income with expenses removed
Income with expenses added into the total

Gross Income is Income before taxes.

What is Debt-to-Income Ratio?

The percentage of a person's monthly earnings used to pay off all debt obligations. Lenders consider two ratios, constructed in slightly different ways. The first called the front-end ratio, the ratio of the monthly housing expenses – including principal, interest, property taxes, and insurance, (PITI) is compared to the borrower's gross, pretax monthly income. In the back-end ratio, a borrower's other debts such as auto loans and credit cards are figured in. Lenders usually consider both and set an acceptable ratio. Some lenders and some lending qualifying agencies only consider the back-end ratio.

The correct formula for factoring a potential mortgage payment is

- Gross Income x 29%
- Net Income x 29%
- Gross Income x 38%
- Net Income x 38%

The correct formula for factoring a potential mortgage payment is gross Income x 29%.

Under conventional loan programs a borrower's monthly payments toward the home should not exceed what percentage of the gross monthly income?

- 25%
- 31%
- 27%
- 29%

Under conventional loan programs a borrower's monthly payments toward the home should not exceed 29% of the gross monthly income.

What is Housing Expense?

The percentage of gross monthly income that goes toward paying a Ratio mortgage or rent on a home.

What notice might you provide an applicant with regard to their credit application?

- Approval
- Counter-offer
- Denial
- Any of the Above

An applicant may receive an Approval, Counter -Offer, or Denial.

Debt to Income is

- The amount of debt a borrower carries
- The amount of income a borrower brings home
- The amount of income a borrower makes before taxes
- None of the above

NONE OF THE ABOVE - Debt to Income is the percentage of the borrower's monthly income that they spend on credit debt.

What is a front-end ratio?

A front-end ratio is the gross income divided by the new PITI mortgage payment.

Which ratio is defined as the gross income divided by the new PITI mortgage payment and the minimum monthly payment from all other liabilities?

- The front end ratio
- The back end ratio
- The debt-to-income ratio
- None of the above

The back end debt ratio is defined as the gross income divided by the new PITI mortgage payment and the minimum monthly payment from all other liabilities.

What methods might you employ to assist in adjusting debt ratios?

- Pay off certain items
- Lower the interest rate of the new loan
- Lower the loan amount offered to the borrower
- Any of the above

If the borrower's debt ratio exceeds the maximum guideline limitations, you cold pay off certain items, lower the interest rate of the new loan or lower the loan amount offered to the borrower to adjust the ratio to meet the guidelines.

Whose income and credit history do you use when calculating debt-to-income ratio for married applicants?

You will use the income and credit history of ALL borrower's on a loan application when calculating debt-to-income ratio.

When a borrower falls just below or on the edge of a credit tier, you may

- Bump them up to the next level
- Request an exception
- Submit every document possible
- None of the above

When a borrower falls just below or on the edge of a credit tier, you may request an exception from underwriting.

The debt ratio will determine

- What loan programs the borrower may obtain
- If the borrower has sufficient monthly income
- How much additional debt a borrower can afford
- All of the above

The debt ratio will determine what loan programs the borrower may obtain, whether the borrower has sufficient monthly income to obtain the loan, and how much additional debt a borrower can afford.

A compensating factor would be

- Larger than minimum down payment
- Credit scores within a few points of the next highest level
- Excellent savings history
- All of the above

A compensating factor would be larger than minimum down payment, credit scores within a few points of the next highest level, and an excellent savings history.

Which monthly liability will not be used to calculate the debt ratio?

- Car Payment
- Child Support
- Utilities
- None of the above

Utilities will not be used to calculate the debt ratio.

A compensating factor is used to

• Exceed normal guidelines
• Subvert normal guidelines
• Coerce the underwriter
• None of the above

A compensating factor is used to exceed normal guidelines.

You will calculate the debt ratio using

• Gross Income
• Net Income
• Additional Income
• None of the above

You will calculate the debt ratio using the borrower's gross income and any additional qualifying income.

What factors may alter the source of funds information entered as the loan process moves toward completion?

- Subordinate finance negotiated
- Seller assistance toward closing costs
- Sales price
- All of the Above

Subordinate finance negotiated between the buyer and seller, seller assistance toward closing costs and the sales price may alter the source of funds information entered as the loan process moves toward completion.

Most loan inquiries are taken

- By the underwriter
- By the Loan Officer
- Over the telephone
- Both B & C

Most loan inquiries are taken by the Loan Officer over the telephone.

The pre-approval questionnaire contains

- All of the information you will need from the borrower
- Most of the information you will need for the loan application
- All of the information the underwriting team will require
- Most of the information necessary to close the loan

The pre-approval questionnaire contains most of the information you will need for the loan application.

The initial contact

- Sets the tone for your relationship with the borrower
- Is the most essential information gathering period
- Sets the loan program you will use for the borrower
- None of the above

The initial contact Sets the tone for your relationship with the borrower.

You may enter common nicknames
for the borrower

- True
- False

You should enter the borrower's full,
legal name. You should not use
common nicknames for the borrower.

You must always have a co-borrower
for the loan

- True
- False

FALSE – A loan application can be
made by one or more individuals.

What is the essential element to gaining the information you need from a borrower?

You must ask for the information.

Why should you request referral information of each pre-qualification?

You should request referral information from each borrower to assist in tracking referral source information, assessing marketing and advertising effectiveness and to provide follow-up information regarding the applicant to the referral source.

Why do you ask if the applicant has chosen a home to purchase during the pre-qualification interview?

- So you can assess the urgency of the query
- To determine if the borrower is working with an agent thereby strengthening referral relationships
- To obtain real purchase numbers for the pre-qualification
- All of the Above

Knowing if the borrower has chosen a home at the time of the initial inquiry enables you to assess the urgency of the query, determine if the borrower is working with an agent thereby strengthening referral relationships, and obtain real purchase numbers for the pre-qualification.

You should complete the pre-qualification questionnaire as soon as the borrower locates the home they wish to purchase.

- True
- False

FALSE - You should complete the pre-qualification questionnaire when the borrower makes the initial inquiry contact.

What is meant by Pre-qualification?

An early evaluation by a lender of a potential homebuyer's credit report, plus earnings, savings, and debt information. The homebuyer gets a non-binding estimate of the mortgage amount the borrower would qualify for, or how much house the borrower can afford. Buyers who pre-qualify can go a step further and seek a pre-approval.

The most important lending product is

- Low rate loans and fixed products
- Professionalism and responsiveness
- Varied products with low down payment
- None of the above

The most important lending product is the professionalism and responsiveness you bring to your customer contacts.

The pre-qualification questionnaire will provide

- answers to every question on the questionnaire
- information that will be noted in the explanation of credit section
- all of the required documentation
- none of the above

Throughout the pre-qualification questionnaire the borrower will provide you with information that will be noted in the explanation of credit section of the questionnaire.

What is an Amortization Schedule?

A timetable for the gradual repayment of a mortgage loan An amortization schedule indicates the amount of each payment applied to interest and principal, and the remaining balance after each payment is made.

Why is it important to include the amortization method planned for a loan package on the initial application?

- It affects the monthly payment
- It affects the debt load
- It dictates the types of disclosures required on an application
- All of the Above

You should include the amortization type planned for the loan on the application because it is a factor in the monthly payment, affects the debt load, and defines some of the required disclosures.

You must always have the subject property address prior to completing the loan application.

A. True
B. False

You can pre-qualify a borrower for a loan amount even if they have not chosen a property to purchase. You will enter "To Be Decided" under the property data fields on the 1003.

Pre-paid items are dictated by

- the sales agreement
- underwriting guidelines
- available funds
- none of the above

Prepaid item requirements will be dictated by underwriting guidelines.

Why would you include borrower income that cannot be used for qualifying purposes on the application?

To assist in modifying DTI Ratios
In case a compensating factor is needed
Approval levels will vary depending on the income of the borrower
Any of the Above

You would include borrower income that cannot be used for qualifying purposes on the application to bring this information to the attention of the underwriter early in the process in order to set the stage for compensating factors in the event an exception is required.

Why is it important to enter information regarding the use the borrower plans to make of the property?

- An occupancy declaration will be required at closing
- A non-owner occupied investment property requires a different application
- Approval levels will vary depending on the occupancy status
- Any of the Above

It is important to enter information regarding the use the borrower plans to make of the property because approval levels will vary depending on the occupancy status of the property.

If a borrower has not chosen a home to purchase, what loan amount do you enter on the 1003?

- "To Be Decided"
- The highest qualifying loan amount
- The lowest qualifying loan amount
- The loan amount that corresponds to the borrower's housing preference

---

The highest qualifying loan amount should be entered because you can easily lower the loan amount later but an increase in the loan amount requested will require the underwriting department to recalculate all numbers and issue a new approval.

The last page of the 1003 may be used for

Employment History
Residence History
Excess Liabilities
Any of the Above

The last page of the 1003 may be used as a continuation sheet for any entry that does not fit within the standard entry fields of the form.

If you do not use the space provided on the continuation sheet page what action should you take?

- Copy the Underwriting Submittal Summary to this area
- Define the compensating factors of the borrower profile
- Cross out the are with an X
- Incorporate additional income into the 1003

The last page of the 1003 may be used as a continuation sheet for any entry that does not fit within the standard entry fields of the form. If additional space is not needed, you should cross out the blank area to assure the borrower that no alterations or additions will be made to the 1003 after the application is signed.

When should you incorporate subordinate financing details into the 1003?

- Upon receipt of the sales agreement
- When the financing terms are finalized
- At the earliest point possible
- Before the closing documents are requested

Including the terms of a subordinate finance agreement early in the process allows the underwriter to approve or decline the terms of subordinate financing before the deal has progressed.

Overtime and bonus income may be used to qualify a borrower providing there is:

A one-year history
A three-year history
A two-year history
A verbal history

Overtime and bonus income may be used to qualify a borrower providing there is a two-year history of receiving this income.

What type of rental income is an acceptable source of income?

- Income from roommates
- Income from boarders
- Income from an investment property received under a lease
- All of the Above

Rental income is an acceptable source of income if it is from an investment property received under a lease.

What percentage of business must a borrower own to be considered self-employed?

- 25%
- 75%
- 90%
- 85%

A borrower can be considered self-employed if they own 25% or more interest in a business.

A borrower may choose to use alimony, child support or separate maintenance if they provide what documentation?

- 12 month payment history from the courts
- Evidence that the payments will continue for at least three years
- Court documents showing who was awarded the largest portion of the overall assets
- Both A & B

A borrower may choose to use alimony, child support or separate maintenance if they provide evidence that the payments will continue for at least three years.

Employment and income do not need to be verified for a non-conventional loan.

- True
- False

Employment and income must be verified on all loan programs except light documentation programs.

Mortgage or rental history is often used to project the probability of a borrower repaying their new mortgage in a timely manner.

- True
- False

TRUE - Mortgage or rental history is often used to project the probability of a borrower repaying their new mortgage in a timely manner.

An outright gift of money toward a purchase of a home is typically acceptable if it is a gift from:

- A charitable organization
- A small loan
- A credit card
- None of the above

An outright gift of money toward a purchase of a home is typically acceptable if it is a gift from a charitable organization.

The down payment for a purchase under HUD guidelines may be obtained as a gift from

- A small local lender
- A family member
- A for profit agency designed to assist in securing down payment funds
- The government

The down payment for a purchase under HUD guidelines may be obtained as a gift from a family member.

What is a CLTV?

- Loan to Value
- Maximum Loan to Value
- Combined Loan to Value
- Cumulative Loan to Value

CLTV
Combined Loan to Value

The method of amortization should
be included on the loan application
because

- It dictates the monthly payment
- It will affect the debt ratios
- It impacts the required disclosures
- All of the above

The method of amortization should be
included on the loan application
because it dictates the monthly
payment, will affect the debt ratios, and
impacts the required disclosures.

Federal Housing Acts have differing
guidelines for

- Single Family Houses
- Multiple unit property
- Second Homes
- All of the above

Federal Housing Acts have differing
guidelines for single family houses,
multiple unit property, and second
homes.

Occupancy Status will effect

- Approval Levels
- Underwriting Schedule
- Appraised Value
- All of the above

Occupancy Status will effect approval levels.

A point is .10 percent of the loan amount

- True
- False

A point is 1% percent of the loan amount.

Non-qualifying income should be
disclosed

- Always
- Only in compensating factor requests
- Only at the request of the borrower
- Never

Non-qualifying income should be
disclosed only at the request of the
borrower.

You must always have the subject
property address prior to completing
the loan application.

- True
- False

FALSE – You may pre-qualify the
borrower for a loan amount enabling
them to choose the property that fits
within the DTI Ratio.

Seller concession toward closing
costs must appear

- On the sales agreement
- Within the loan application
- On the settlement statement
- All of the above

Seller concession toward closing costs
must appear on the sales agreement,
within the loan application, and on the
settlement statement.

It is a portion of your job function to assist
borrowers in determining the source of
funds to be used in a transaction.

- True
- False

TRUE - It is a portion of your job
function to assist borrowers in
determining the source of funds to be
used in a transaction.

The appraisal will be used for

- Equity assessment
- Title insurance
- LTV Assessment
- All of the above

The appraisal will be used for a variety of loan aspects including equity assessment, title insurance and LTV assessment.

The property in a loan process is as important a factor as borrower history

- True
- False

TRUE – The property serves as collateral to enable the lender to regain their investment if the borrower defaults on the mortgage loan.

URAR is an abbreviation for

- The Uniform Residential Appraisal Report
- The 1004
- The most common appraisal you will encounter
- All of the above

URAR is an abbreviation for for Uniform Residential Appraisal Report, the most common appraisal you will encounter. The form number of the URAR is 1004.

What is a red flag?

A red flag is any information that appears regarding issues that will stand in the way of the completion of the loan.

What are Comparables?

The term comparables efers to "comparable properties" which are used for comparative purposes in the appraisal process. Comps are recently sold properties that are similar in size, location, and amenities to the home for sale. Comps help an appraiser determine the fair market value of a property.

The appraiser will note Red Flags during the appraisal process

- True
- False

TRUE - The appraiser will note Red Flags during the appraisal process.

The appraiser will assess

- The property
- The neighborhood
- Recently sold property
- All of the above

The appraiser will assess the property, neighborhood, and recently sold property to determine the market value of the subject property.

Why is it important to locate red flags early in the process?

It is sometimes more effective and a faster process to request the necessary correction items or additional information immediately rather than waiting for the underwriter to generate a stipulation regarding the matter.

You should never read the appraisal before underwriting

- True
- False

FALSE – You should review the appraisal to note any errors that need to be corrected or red flag issues that may need to be overcome before the loan can close.

What is your goal when reviewing an appraisal?

You should review the appraisal to scrutinize any item that appears to vary between documents in the file and the entries on the appraisal to determine which document contains the error and to note any item that is below the minimum requirements of the loan guideline, which you are planning for the loan file.

If you note a discrepancy, error or issue on the appraisal report you should

- Notify underwriting
- Influence the appraiser to alter the item
- Notify the appraiser of the issue
- Request a field review appraisal

If you note a discrepancy, error or issue on the appraisal report you should notify the appraiser of the issue. You should not request that the appraiser make any changes to the value or to the specific inclusions of the appraisal. You should only contact the appraiser if there is an error on the document.

What alterations should you make to a completed appraisal if you discover an issue during your review?

You should only request alterations arising because of an error or omission not an alteration to the opinion or decision of the appraiser.

Property Valuation will be determined by

- Comparison with other property
- Sales price of other property
- Proximity to recently sold property
- All of the above

Property Valuation will be determined by comparison with other property, sales price of other property, and proximity of the subject property to recently sold property.

What does the sales comparison valuation approach consider?

The sales comparison approach assesses the characteristics of the subject property as compared to other similar properties sold within a given time period.

You must place each loan carefully because there are a limited number of loan products to choose from

- True
- False

FALSE – There are many loan products available and you should select the one that best suits the needs of the borrower.

A product matrix is

- The final underwriting guideline manual
- A snapshot of minimum requirements
- A snapshot of final requirements
- None of the above

A product matrix is a snapshot of minimum requirements of the loan program.

A product matrix will allow you to assess a loans suitability for your borrower.

- True
- False

TRUE - A product matrix will allow you to assess a loans suitability for your borrower.

What is Loan-to-value (LTV) Ratio ?

The ratio of a mortgage loan amount to the property's appraised value or selling price, whichever is less For example, if a home is sold for $100,000 and the mortgage amount is $80,000 the LTV is 80%.

You will begin grading using

- The loan application
- The pre-qualification questionnaire
- The credit-scoring key
- The borrower history

You will begin grading using the pre-qualification questionnaire.

The second step in loan pricing is

- Review the pay structure for each pricing category
- Review the maximum qualifying criteria for each pricing category
- Determine the borrower's DTI
- Any of the Above

The second step in pricing the loan is to review the maximum qualifying guidelines on the rate sheet to determine which approval level meets the inclusions of the borrower profile.

You will need to compare

- At least one decisioning factor
- All decisioning factors
- Specific decisioning factors
- None of the above

You will need to compare all decisioning factors on the product matrix against the borrower's situation.

What is a pricing restriction?

A pricing restriction is an internal limitation or requirement and applicable laws regarding loan pricing.

You should begin grading

- At the lowest approval tier
- At the highest approval tier
- At the highest paying approval level
- At the bottom of the matrix

You should begin grading at the highest approval tier and work downwards until you find the program that meets your borrower's qualifications.

You may exceed an approval level by

- Changing the credit report
- Speaking to underwriting
- Supplying adequate compensating factors
- Never

You may exceed an approval level by supplying adequate compensating factors.

If the housing expense exceeds the loan criteria you must

- Move on to the next loan matrix
- Suggest alternative options to the borrower
- Request underwriting change the matrix
- None of the above

If the housing expense exceeds the loan criteria you must move onto another loan product or suggest alternatives to the borrower including a lower purchase price, alterative loan program, or the application of discount points.

What must you determine prior to beginning the actual pricing?

- Preferred loan terms
- The LTV required
- Pricing including office payment
- All of the Above

Prior to beginning the actual pricing you must determine the borrower's preferred loan terms, the LTV required, and the pricing including office payment.

Who is the best candidate for a fixed rate program?

- Perpetual high-risk borrower
- Long-term purchaser
- Cautious borrower
- All of the Above

A perpetual high-risk borrower, a long-term purchaser or a cautious borrower are all good candidates for a fixed rate program.

What does it mean to price at PAR?

- To wrap a point into the rate
- To wrap no points into the rate
- To wrap all points into the rate
- None of the Above

Pricing at PAR means that there are no points wrapped in the interest rate.

When pricing a loan you should use

- The rate sheet that generates the most income for your branch
- The most current rate sheet
- The rate sheet provided by your branch manager
- None of the above

When pricing a loan you should use the most current rate sheet.

Pricing restrictions may occur as a result of

- Internal requirements
- Applicable laws
- Pre-payment penalty
- All of the above

Pricing restrictions may occur as a result of internal requirements, applicable laws, and pre-payment penalty application.

All rate sheets will include qualifying information for you to review

- True
- False

FALSE – Not all rate sheets will include qualifying information for you to review

---

What pre-pay terms do most lenders offer?

- 2-year
- 3-year
- 5-year
- All of the above

Many lenders offer 0, 2, 3, and 5-year penalties

You will determine the interest rate offered using

- The loan term
- The LTV
- The branch income
- All of the Above

You will determine the interest rate offered using the loan term, LTV, and the branch income.

The use of a pre-payment penalty may

- Impact the final rate
- Generate additional branch income
- Violate regulations
- All of the above

The use of a pre-payment penalty may impact the final rate, generate additional branch income, and violate regulations.

What the most common written decision you will see from underwriting?

- Approved
- Conditional
- Denied
- Any of the Above

Underwriting may issue a determination that the application is approved, conditional, or denied.

What is a Pre-Approval?

This process goes a step further than pre-qualification. It means the lender has contacted the borrower's employer, bank, and other places to verify all claims of earnings and assets. In return, the borrower receives a letter stating the lender is willing to grant a mortgage for a specific amount within a limited period with the stipulation that there are no material changes to the borrower's situation.

The loan officer is the liaison between

- The borrower and underwriting
- The borrower and the loan funder
- The broker and underwriting
- The lender and the broker

The loan officer is the liaison between the borrower and underwriting.

What is Disbursement ?

The release of funds held in an escrow account.

Each time you submit a stipulation
the underwriter will

- Review the entire loan file
- Request additional documentation
- Complain about the documentation
- Request a different stipulation

Each time you submit a stipulation the
underwriter will review the entire loan
file.

If you must repeatedly return to the
borrower for additional
documentation you will gain

- Borrower loyalty
- A poor reputation
- Underwriting approval
- All of the above

If you must repeatedly return to the
borrower for additional documentation
you will gain a poor reputation.

The underwriting summary is a form of

- Checklist of Inclusions
- Guideline
- Application Overview
- None of the Above

The underwriting summary is a checklist of inclusions.

What is Closing?

The meeting at which the sale of a property is finalized. The buyer signs the lender agreement for the mortgage and pays' closing costs and escrow amounts. The buyer and seller sign documents to transfer the ownership of the property. Also known as the settlement.

When requesting an appraisal you should note

- The borrower's approval rating
- The method of billing and payment
- The title company who will close the loan
- The possibility of a field review

When requesting an appraisal you should note the method of billing and payment. The appraisal will want to collect a 'pay at the door' payment when they complete the appraisal.

The most important product a Loan Officer has available is

- Low interest rates
- Fast underwriting approvals
- Customer service skills
- The ability to relate well to borrowers

The most important product a Loan Officer has available are customer service skills. A borrower will become a repeat borrower and a referral source if you use your customer service skills to build a solid and positive relationship.

The first act you will take on a loan package is to

- Pull the credit report
- Review the application
- Complete the pre-qualification
- Send VOE/VOR/VOM forms

The first act you will take on a loan package is to complete the pre-qualification.

What is the Title Search?

A check of title records to ensure that the seller is the legal owner of a property and that there are no liens or other claims against the property.

You should revise the good faith
estimate

- Frequently throughout the loan
  process
- Upon altering any loan specifics
- Upon receipt of the sales agreement
- Upon receipt of the initial loan
  approval

You should revise the good faith
estimate if you alter any loan specifics.

What is a Good Faith Estimate?

A written estimate of closing costs that
the lender must provide to prospective
homebuyers within three days of
submitting a mortgage loan
application.

The borrower should be informed of the final loan specifics

- Before the closing
- The day of closing
- At the closing table
- None of the above

The borrower should be informed of the final loan specifics before the closing.

What is Hazard Insurance?

Insurance coverage that compensates for physical damage to property from natural disasters such as fire and other hazards Depending on where a piece of property is located, lenders may also require flood insurance or policies covering windstorms (hurricanes) or earthquakes

The underwriter will review all aspects of the file including:

- Source of down payment
- The borrower's credit history
- The borrower's compensating factors
- All of the above

The underwriter will review all aspects of the file including source of down payment, the borrower's compensating factors, the borrower's credit history.

What are PITI Reserves?

A cash amount that a homebuyer must have on hand after making a down payment and paying all closing costs   The reserves required by a lender must equal the amount a buyer would pay for PITI for a specific number of months.

Prior to closing conditions must be provided to the underwriter before the loan documents can be requested.

- True
- False

TRUE – The underwriter must clear all prior to close conditions before the loan documents will be issued.

The processing stage is a stage where

- All information is verified and submitted
- Missing documentation is requested
- All loan specifics are finalized
- All of the above

The processing stage is a stage where all information is verified, documentation is submitted to underwriting, missing documentation is requested, and all loan specifics are finalized.

A verification of deposit is a form sent

- To the closing or settlement agent to verify the funds to close
- To the bank to verify the average bank account balance of the borrower
- To the real estate agent to verify the earnest money deposit
- None of the above

A verification of deposit is a form sent to the bank to verify the average bank account balance of the borrower.

What are Closing Costs?

Expenses incurred by buyers and sellers in transferring ownership of a property. Closing costs normally include an origination fee, an attorney's fee, taxes, escrow payments, and charges for title insurance. Lenders or Real Estate Agents provide estimates of closing costs to prospective homebuyers.

The funding is when

- The underwriter completes a final loan review
- The monies borrowed are wired or sent to the closing agent
- The monies borrowed are disbursed to the proper individuals
- None of the Above

The funding is when the monies borrowed are wired or sent to the closing agent.

Many loan officers forget to create

- A good closing team
- An adequate filing system
- Positive service relationships
- Borrower commitment

Many loan officers forget to create positive service relationships.

An affinity service provider includes any individual who must accomplish tasks in a timely and professional manner in order for you to accomplish your goal of closed loans.

- True
- False

TRUE - An affinity service provider includes any individual who must accomplish tasks in a timely and professional manner in order for you to accomplish your goal of closed loans.

You should treat your affinity service providers

- Respectfully
- Friendly
- With Consideration
- All of the above

You should treat your affinity service providers with respect and consideration to help foster positive affinity service relationships.

Skill Enhancement Self-Tests

Section

2

Name
Loan Officer Review Questions
Fundamentals
Instructor:
Score:

1.   What are the two classifications within the mortgage market?

_____

_____

_____

_____

_____

2.   What is an investing pool?

_____

_____

_____

_____

_____

3.   What are the three most common employment opportunities for a loan officer?

_____

_____

_____

_____

_____

_____

4.   What is the purpose of a mortgage brokerage? _____

_____

_____

_____

_____

_____

5.   What are the most common entities within the secondary mortgage market/

_____

_____

_____

_____

_____

6.   Which is not a common entity within the primary mortgage market?
        a.   Mortgage Brokerage Office
        b.   Mutual Savings Bank
        c.   Credit Union
        d.   Insurance Company

Name
Loan Officer Review Questions
Fundamentals - Ethics and Disclosure
Instructor:
Score:

1.   What is the purpose of the laws that govern the ethics and disclosures with which you
        handle loan processes?

_____

_____

_____

_____

_____

2.   What is HMDA?

_____

_____

_____

_____

_____

3.   What is the purpose of fair housing laws?

_____

_____

_____

_____

_____

4. What other act assists in the prevention of discrimination against applicants?

_____

_____

_____

_____

_____

5. What items are illegal for use in evaluating applicant's qualifications?

_____

_____

_____

_____

_____

6. What are the three common notices you might provide an applicant with regard to their credit application?

_____

_____

_____

_____

_____

7. What is RESPA?

_____

_____

_____

_____

_____

8.   What is the disclosure notice requirement if a loan is transferred to a new servicer?

_____

_____

_____

_____

_____

9.   What is a settlement statement?

_____

_____

_____

_____

_____

10.   What is TILA?

_____

_____

_____

_____

_____

11.   When must a right to cancel be provided?

_____

_____

_____

_____

_____

_____

12. Explain the reason for HOEPA.

_____

_____

_____

_____

_____

13. When will PMI be automatically cancelled in a normal risk mortgage?

_____

_____

_____

_____

_____

14. When will PMI be automatically cancelled in a high-risk mortgage?

_____

_____

_____

_____

_____

15. What is HUD and what is their function?

_____

_____

_____

_____

_____

16. What is PMI?

_____

_____

_____

_____

_____

17. What is the annual mortgage-insurance premium?

_____

_____

_____

_____

18   Why have ethics and disclosure laws been created?

    a.   To provide the lender with a series of practical directions

    b.   To protect the interest of the public

    c.   To make the obtainment of mortgage funds a fair practice

    d.   All of the above

19. The Loan Officer must:

    a.   educate the consumer

    b.   act in an ethical manner

    c.   incorporate the required practices into their daily workload

    d.   all of the above

20. Many states have created educational and licensure requirements for lending professionals.

    a.   True

    b.   False

21. HMDA requires the reporting of
    a. pipeline reports
    b. loan origination referral data
    c. public loan data
    d. none of the above

22. Information for the HMDA reports should be gathered:
    a. at the closing table
    b. at the time of pre-qualification
    c. at the initial application
    d. during post-close processes

23. Fair housing laws are designed to prevent
    a. discrimination in a credit related transaction
    b. discrimination in the setting of application appointments
    c. too many underprivileged loan disbursements
    d. none of the above

24. ECOA is
    a. equal credit origination act
    b. every credit opportunity agenda
    c. equal credit opportunity act
    d. none of the above

25. ECOA addresses:
    a. discriminatory actions
    b. predatory lending tactics
    c. required action disclosures
    d. all of the above

26. RESPA

    a.   Helps consumers shop for settlement services

    b.   Eliminates referral fees

    c.   Requires specific borrower disclosures

    d.   All of the above

27. A point is .10 percent of the loan amount

    a.   True

    b.   False

28. The borrower has the right to cancel any credit transaction involving their home within 3 days of the funding of the transaction.

    a.   True

    b.   False

29. All borrowers must purchase flood insurance

    a.   True

    b.   False

30. HUD is a direct lender

    a.   True

    b.   False

Name
Loan Officer Review Questions
Fundamentals – Documentation
Instructor:
Score:

1.   Why is it important to document each loan package you submit?

_____

_____

_____

_____

_____

2.   Why should you note any missing information on the loan cover letter that you submit with the package?

_____

_____

_____

_____

_____

3.   Why should you include compensating factor information at the time of the initial submittal even when an exception request is not expected?

_____

_____

_____

_____

_____

4. Why should you include information regarding the approval and transaction specifics you are requesting as part of your loan cover sheet?

_____

_____

_____

_____

_____

5. What is the purpose of a stipulation list?

_____

_____

_____

_____

_____

6. What are the three common written decisions you will see from underwriting?

_____

_____

_____

_____

_____

7. What is an affinity provider?

_____

_____

_____

_____

_____

8. Who is ultimately responsible for the smooth process and timely closing of the loan?

_____

_____

_____

_____

_____

9. How can you avoid loan process delays?

_____

_____

_____

_____

_____

10. How can you foster positive relationships with affinity service providers?

_____

_____

_____

_____

_____

11. Why must you request income documentation from each borrower?

_____

_____

_____

_____

_____

12.   What does the mortgage or rental history tell the loan underwriter?

_____

_____

_____

_____

_____

_____

13.   What is a VOM?

_____

_____

_____

_____

_____

14.   What is a CLTV?

_____

_____

_____

_____

_____

15.   Explain the general rule regarding credit risk and borrower investment.

_____

_____

_____

_____

_____

16. Why should you request all borrower documentation at the beginning of the loan process?

_____

_____

_____

_____

_____

17. Overtime and bonus income may be used to qualify a borrower providing there is:

    a.   A one-year history

    b.   A three-year history

    c.   A two-year history

    d.   A verbal history

18. What type of rental income is an acceptable source of income?

    a.   Income from roommates

    b.   Income from boarders

    c.   Rent received by parents

    d.   Income from an investment property received under a lease

19. What percentage of business must a borrower own to be considered self-employed?

    a.   25%

    b.   75%

    c.   90%

    d.   85%

20. A borrower may choose to use alimony, child support, or separate maintenance if they provide what documentation?

   a.   12 month payment history from the courts

   b.   Evidence that the payments will continue for at least three years

   c.   Court documents showing who was awarded the largest portion of the overall assets

   d.   Both A & B

21. Mortgage or rental history is often used to project the probability of a borrower repaying their new mortgage in a timely manner.

   a.   True

   b.   False

22. If the mortgage or rental history is not included in the credit report, which of the following is an acceptable replacement?

   a.   Verification forms sent to the mortgage holder or rental management company, if these are an entity not an individual to verify the history of the account

   b.   A letter from the landlord or mortgage holder saying the rent or mortgage payment was received in a timely manner

   c.   12 months cancelled rent checks showing a timely payment to an individual landlord or mortgage holder

   d.   Both A & C

23. Bank statement as income documentation programs are typically not penalized with a higher interest or down payment requirement because the statements are considered full documentation.

   a.   True

   b.   False

24. An outright gift of money toward a purchase of a home is typically acceptable if it is a gift from:

    a. A charitable organization

    b. A small loan

    c. A credit card

    d. None of the above

25. The loan officer is the liaison between

    a. the borrower and the loan funder

    b. the borrower and underwriting

    c. the broker and underwriting

    d. the lender and the broker

26. Each time you submit a stipulation the underwriter will

    a. review the entire loan file

    b. request additional documentation

    c. complain about the documentation

    d. request a different stipulation

27. If you must repeatedly return to the borrower for additional documentation, you will gain

    a. borrower loyalty

    b. a poor reputation

    c. underwriting approval

    d. all of the above

28. The underwriting summary is a form of
   a. checklist of inclusions
   b. guideline
   c. application overview
   d. none of the above

29. When requesting an appraisal you should note
   a. the borrowers approval rating
   b. the method of billing and payment
   c. the title company who will close the loan
   d. the possibility of a field review

30. The most important product a Loan Officer has available is
   a. low interest rates
   b. fast underwriting approvals
   c. customer service skills
   d. the ability to relate well to borrowers

31. The first act you will take on a loan package is to
   a. pull the credit report
   b. review the application
   c. complete the pre-qualification
   d. send VOE/VOR/VOM forms

32. You should revise the good faith estimate
   a. frequently throughout the loan process
   b. upon altering any borrower credit specifics
   c. upon receipt of the sales agreement
   d. upon receipt of the initial loan approval

33. The borrower should be informed of the final loan specifics

    a.   before the closing

    b.   the day of closing

    c.   at the closing table

    d.   none of the above

34. The loan officer should take gifts to the closing

    a.   True

    b.   False

35. The underwriter will review all aspects of the file including:

    a.   Source of down payment

    b.   The borrower's personal recommendations

    c.   The borrower's professional references

    d.   All of the above

36. The underwriter will review the file and issue an

    a.   approval

    b.   denial

    c.   conditional approval

    d.   Any of the above

37. Prior to closing documents must be provided to the underwriter before the loan documents can be requested.

    a.   True

    b.   False

38. The processing stage is a stage where
    a. all information is verified and submitted
    b. missing documentation is requested
    c. data is transferred to the underwriter
    d. all of the above

39. A verification of deposit is a form sent
    a. To the closing or settlement agent to verify the funds to close
    b. To the bank to verify the average bank account balance of the borrower
    c. to the real estate agent to verify the earnest money deposit
    d. none of the above

40. The funding is when
    a. the underwriter completes a final loan review
    b. the monies borrowed are wired or sent to the closing agent
    c. the monies borrowed are disbursed to the proper individuals
    d. none of the above

41. Delays in the loan process can be avoided by
    a. implementing a loan process follow-up and reminder system
    b. creating strong relationships with affinity service providers
    c. efficient pipeline management
    d. all of the above

42. Many loan officers forget to create
    a. a good closing team
    b. an adequate filing system
    c. positive service relationships
    d. borrower commitment

43. An affinity service provider includes any individual who must accomplish tasks in a timely and professional manner in order for you to accomplish your goal of closed loans.

    a.   True

    b.   False

44. You should treat your affinity service providers

    a.   Respectfully

    b.   Friendly

    c.   With Consideration

    d.   All of the above

Name
Loan Officer Review Questions
Fundamentals - Prequalification
Instructor:
Score:

1.   What is the primary reason that many loan Officers fail to obtain the information that
        will be needed for a pre-qualification?

_____

_____

_____

_____

_____

2.   What is the essential element to gaining the information you need from a borrower?

_____

_____

_____

_____

_____

3.   Why is the initial contact with any potential borrower important?

_____

_____

_____

_____

_____

4. Why should you request referral information of each pre-qualification?

_____

_____

_____

_____

_____

5. Why do you ask if the applicant has chosen a home to purchase during the pre-qualification interview?

_____

_____

_____

_____

_____

6. What is your most important product?

_____

_____

_____

_____

_____

7. Most loan inquiries are taken
   a. by the underwriter
   b. by the loan Officer
   c. over the telephone
   d. both b & c

8.	Your most valuable tool in planning a loan strategy is
	a.	customer service skills
	b.	information
	c.	qualification skills
	d.	loan knowledge

9.	The pre-approval questionnaire contains
	a.	all of the information you will need from the borrower
	b.	most of the information you will need for the loan application
	c.	all of the information the underwriting team will require
	d.	most of the information necessary to close the loan

10.	The initial contact
	a.	sets the tone for your relationship with the borrower
	b.	is the most essential information-gathering period
	c.	sets the loan program you will use for the borrower
	d.	none of the above

11.	You will request a credit authorization verbally before pulling borrower credit.
	a.	True
	b.	False

12.	You may enter common nicknames for the borrower
	a.	True
	b.	False

13.	You must always have a co-borrower for the loan
	a.	True
	b.	False

14. You should complete the pre-qualification questionnaire as soon as the borrower locates the home they wish to purchase

    a. True

    b. False

15. The most important lending product is

    a. low rate loans and fixed products

    b. professionalism and responsiveness

    c. varied products with low down payment

    d. none of the above

16. The pre-qualification questionnaire will provide you with

    a. answers to every question on the questionnaire

    b. information that will be noted in the explanation of credit section

    c. all of the required documentation

    d. none of the above

Name
Loan Officer Review Questions
Practice – Reading the Credit Report
Instructor:
Score:

1. What does a credit report show about a borrower?

_____

_____

_____

_____

_____

2. What is your primary concern when reviewing a borrower's credit report?

_____

_____

_____

_____

_____

3. What is the score range you can expect to see on a credit report?

_____

_____

_____

_____

_____

4. What are the three credit bureaus you will encounter?

_____

_____

_____

_____

_____

5. What is a FICO?

_____

_____

_____

_____

_____

6. How is the FICO generated?

_____

_____

_____

_____

_____

7. Fair, Isaac credit bureau scores do NOT use what as predictive characteristics:

_____

_____

_____

_____

_____

8. What do credit bureau scores provide to a lender?

_____

_____

_____

_____

_____

9.   How can you gain information to assist you in understanding why a credit report scored the way it did?

_____

_____

_____

_____

_____

_____

10.   Credit Reports are:
      A.   A great way to see how many things people buy
      B.   A way to get to know a borrower's likes and dislikes
      C.   An overview of a person's entire history of spending and payment
      D.   None of the above

11   Credit reports are an overview of a person's entire history of spending and payment habits.
      A.   True
      B.   False

12.   A bankruptcy can remain on a credit report for
      A.   3 years
      B.   7 years
      C.   10 years
      D.   Life

13.   Accounts to medical services that a borrower has failed to pay as agreed are
      A.   Often treated differently
      B.   Never a concern
      C.   An underwriting condition
      D.   Always to be paid in full

14.   Repeatedly requesting a borrower's credit report may
      A.   Adversely effect the credit score
      B.   Show the borrower's can obtain further credit
      C.   Cause an underwriting condition
      D.   All of the above

15. A late payment is any payment paid past the due date even when within the grace period
    A.   True
    B.   False

16. Credit bureau scores are based upon
    A.   Every action taken by a borrower with regard to debt
    B.   The data contained within the credit bureau
    C.   All information contained within the loan application
    D.   None of the above

17 A credit bureau score will rank order potential borrowers based upon the number of good loans to bad loans.
    A.   True
    B.   False

Name
Loan Officer Review Questions
Practice – Compensating Factors and DTI
Instructor:
Score:

1. What is a compensating factor? _____

_____

_____

_____

_____

_____

2. Why do you use compensating factors? _____

_____

_____

_____

_____

_____

3. Name three potential compensating factors: _____

_____

_____

_____

_____

_____

4. What does a debt ratio tell you about a file? _____

_____

_____

_____

_____

_____

5. What is a front-end ratio? _____

_____

_____

_____

_____

_____

6. Which ratio is defined as the gross income divided by the new PITI mortgage payment and the minimum monthly payment from all other liabilities? _____

_____

_____

_____

_____

_____

7. Name three items not commonly factored into the debt ratio: _____

_____

_____

_____

_____

_____

8. What are three methods that you might employ to assist in adjusting debt ratios? _____

_____

_____

_____

_____

_____

9. How many times do you factor each debt when calculating debt ratios?

_____

_____

_____

_____

_____

9. Whose income and credit history do you use when calculating debt-to-income ratio for married applicants?

_____

_____

_____

_____

_____

11. Explain the premise of debt-to-income ratios.

_____

_____

_____

_____

_____

12. Gross income is:

_____

_____

_____

_____

_____

13.   Explain the formula for factoring a potential mortgage payment.

_____

_____

_____

_____

_____

14.   What is a compensating factor and why is it important?

_____

_____

_____

_____

_____

15.   When a borrower falls just below or on the edge of a credit tier, you may
       A. Bump them up to the next level
       B. Request an exception
       C. Submit every document possible
       D. None of the above

16.   The debt ratio will determine
       A. What loan programs the borrower may obtain
       B. If the borrower has sufficient monthly income
       C. How much additional debt a borrower can afford
       D. All of the above

17.   Which monthly liability will not be used to calculate the debt ratio?
       A. Car Payment
       B. Child Support
       C. Utilities
       D. None of the above

18.   The Debt-to-Income Ratio can be adjusted if
       A. There are items that can be paid off
       B. The interest rate can be lowered
       C. There are items that will be paid in full within 4 months
       D. All of the above

19. A compensating factor would be
    A. Larger than minimum down payment
    B. Credit scores within a few points of the next highest level
    C. Excellent savings history
    D. All of the above

20. A compensating factor is used to
    A. Exceed normal guidelines
    B. Subvert normal guidelines
    C. Coerce the underwriter
    D. None of the above

21. You will calculate the debt ratio using
    A. Gross Income
    B. Net Income
    C. Additional Income
    D. None of the above

22. The ability to borrow more money is affected by
    A.   How much debt potential a borrower currently carries
    B.   How many things a borrower has in his house
    C.   How a borrower treats you and your company
    D.   All of the above

23. Debt to Income is
    A.   The amount of debt a borrower carries
    B.   The amount of income a borrower brings home
    C.   The amount of income a borrower makes before taxes
    D.   None of the above

Name
Loan Officer Review Questions
Practice – The Loan Application
Instructor:
Score:

1.   Why is it important to include the amortization method planned for a loan package on the initial application?

_____

_____

_____

_____

2.   What is the appropriate entry on the application if a borrower is applying for a pre-approval with no property in mind?

_____

_____

_____

_____

3.   Why is it important to enter information regarding the use the borrower plans to make of the property?

_____

_____

_____

_____

4.   What factors may alter the source of funds information entered as the loan process moves toward completion?

_____

_____

_____

_____

_____

5.   What action should you take if you need additional space to reference residence history, employment history, debt information or other borrower specific information that needs to be included in the application?

_____

_____

_____

_____

_____

6.   Why would you include borrower income that cannot be used for qualifying purposes on the application?

_____

_____

_____

_____

_____

7.   What monthly payment amount will you enter for a revolving liability that currently has not balance?

_____

_____

_____

_____

_____

8.   What is the premise behind requesting the highest loan amount that a borrower will
      be eligible to receive when submitting for a pre-approval that has no actual subject
      property?

      _____

      _____

      _____

      _____

      _____

9.   Why should you include any information you have regarding possible subordinate
      financing early in the approval process?

      _____

      _____

      _____

      _____

      _____

10.   If you do not use the space provided on the continuation sheet page what action
      should you take?

      _____

      _____

      _____

      _____

      _____

11.   The method of amortization should be included on the loan application because
      A. It dictates the monthly payment
      B. It will affect the debt ratios
      C. It affects the required disclosures
      D. All of the above

12.   You must always have the subject property address prior to completing the loan
      application.
      A. True
      B. False

13. Federal Housing Acts have differing guidelines for
    A. Single Family Houses
    B. Multiple unit property
    C. Second Homes
    D. All of the above

14. Occupancy Status will effect
    A. Approval Levels
    B. Underwriting Schedule
    C. Appraised Value
    D. All of the above

15. It is a portion of your job function to assist borrowers in determining the source of funds to be used in a transaction.
    A. True
    B. False

16. Non-qualifying income should be disclosed
    A. Always
    B. Only in compensating factor requests
    C. Only at the request of the borrower
    D. Never

17. Pre-paid items are dictated by
    A. the sales agreement
    B. underwriting guidelines
    C. available funds
    D. none of the above

18. Seller concession toward closing costs must appear
    A. on the sales agreement
    B. within the loan application
    C. on the settlement statement
    D. all of the above

Name
Loan Officer Review Questions
Practice - Appraisals
Instructor:
Score:

1.   Why is an appraisal vital to the loan process?

_____

_____

_____

_____

_____

2.   What is a red flag?

_____

_____

_____

_____

_____

3.   What is URAR?

_____

_____

_____

_____

_____

4.   What is your goal when reviewing an appraisal?

_____

_____

_____

_____

_____

5.   What action should you take if you discover an error in a loan document?

_____

_____

_____

_____

_____

6.   Why is it important to locate red flags early in the process?

_____

_____

_____

_____

7.   What alterations should you make to a completed appraisal if you discover an issue during your review?

_____

_____

_____

_____

_____

8.   What does the sales comparison valuation approach consider?

_____

_____

_____

_____

_____

9.   The property in a loan process is as important a factor as borrower history
A. True
B. False

10. The appraisal will be used for
    A. Equity assessment
    B. Title insurance
    C. LTV Assessment
    D. All of the above

11. URAR is an abbreviation for
    A. The Uniform Residential Appraisal Report
    B. The 1004
    C. The most common appraisal you will encounter
    D. All of the above

12. The appraiser will note Red Flags during the appraisal process
    A. True
    B. False

13. The appraiser will assess
    A. The property
    B. The neighborhood
    C. Recently sold property
    D. All of the above

14. You should never read the appraisal before underwriting
    A. True
    B. False

15. If you note a discrepancy, error or issue on the appraisal report you should
    A. Notify underwriting
    B. Influence the appraiser to alter the item
    C. Notify the appraiser of the issue
    D. Request a field review appraisal

16. Property Valuation will be determined by
    A. Comparison with other property
    B. Sales price of other property
    C. Proximity to recently sold property
    D. All of the above

1. Why is it important to become familiar with the guidelines of the various loan products available through your branch?

_____

_____

_____

_____

_____

2. What is a product matrix?

_____

_____

_____

_____

_____

3. What is the first step in grading a package for loan placement?

_____

_____

_____

_____

_____

4. What factor may alter the pricing you initially plan for a loan placement?

_____

_____

_____

_____

5.　What are some steps you might take if the new loan causes the borrower to exceed the ratio limitations set by the loan guidelines?

_____

_____

_____

_____

_____

6.　You must place each loan carefully because there are a limited number of loan products to choose from

   A. True
   B. False

7.　A product matrix is

   A. The final underwriting guideline manual
   B. A snapshot of minimum requirements
   C. A snapshot of final requirements
   D None of the above

8.　A product matrix will allow you to assess a loans suitability for your borrower.

   A. True
   B. False

9.　You will begin grading using

   A. The loan application
   B. The pre-qualification questionnaire
   C. The credit-scoring key
   D　The borrower history

10.　You will need to compare

   A. At least one decisioning factor
   B. All decisioning factors
   C. Specific decisioning factors
   D. None of the above

11. You should begin grading

   A. At the lowest approval tier
   B. At the highest approval tier
   C. At the highest paying approval level
   D At the bottom of the matrix

12. You may exceed an approval level by

   A. Changing the credit report
   B. Speaking to underwriting
   C. Supplying adequate compensating factors
   D. Never

13. If the housing expense exceeds the loan criteria, you must

   A. Move on to the next loan matrix
   B. Suggest alternative options to the borrower
   C. Request underwriting change the matrix
   D None of the above

Name
Loan Officer Review Questions
Practice – Pricing the Loan
Instructor:
Score:

1. What is a pricing restriction? _____

_____

_____

_____

_____

_____

2. What is the second step in loan pricing? _____

_____

_____

_____

_____

_____

3. What three items must you determine prior to beginning the actual pricing? _____

_____

_____

_____

_____

4. Who is the best candidate for a fixed rate program?

_____

_____

_____

_____

_____

5. What is a prepayment penalty?

_____

_____

_____

_____

_____

6. What common pre-pay terms do most lenders offer?

_____

_____

_____

_____

_____

7. What benefit does the pre-payment penalty offer to a lender?

_____

_____

_____

_____

_____

8. What is the primary benefit to the use of a pre-pay penalty for the borrower?

_____

_____

_____

_____

_____

9. What does it mean to price at PAR?

_____

_____

_____

_____

_____

10. When do you use the Margin?

_____

_____

_____

_____

_____

11. When pricing a loan you should use
   A. The rate sheet that generates the most income for your branch
   B. The most current rate sheet
   C. The rate sheet provided by your branch manager
   D. None of the above

12. Pricing restrictions may occur as a result of
   A. Internal requirements
   B. Applicable laws
   C. Pre-payment penalty
   D. All of the above

13.	All rate sheets will include qualifying information for you to review
	A. True
	B. False

14.	You will determine the interest rate offered using
	A. The loan term
	B. The LTV
	C. The branch income
	D. All of the above

15.	The pre-payment requirements may
	A. Impact the final rate
	B. Generate additional branch income
	C. Violate regulations

KEY TERMS AND DEFINITIONS

Use the knowledge you have obtained from the text to provide the definition of the terms.

1.   Closing costs:

_____

_____

_____

_____

_____

_____

2.   VA Mortgage:

_____

_____

_____

_____

_____

3.   Amortization Schedule:

_____

_____

_____

_____

_____

4.   Closing:

_____

_____

_____

_____

_____

5.   Title search: _____

_____

_____

_____

_____

_____

6.   Disbursement: _____

_____

_____

_____

_____

_____

7.   Credit report: _____

_____

_____

_____

_____

_____

8.   Acceleration Clause: _____

_____

_____

_____

_____

_____

9.   Loan-to-value (LTV) Ratio:

_____

_____

_____

_____

_____

_____

10.   Housing Expense:

_____

_____

_____

_____

_____

_____

11.   Pre-approval:

_____

_____

_____

_____

_____

_____

12.   Good Faith Estimate:

_____

_____

_____

_____

_____

13.   Freddie Mac:

_____
_____
_____
_____
_____

14.   Debt-to-Income Ratio:

_____
_____
_____
_____
_____

15.   Comparables:

_____
_____
_____
_____

16.   RESPA:

_____
_____
_____
_____
_____

17. Pre-qualification:

_____

_____

_____

_____

_____

_____

18. PITI Reserves:

_____

_____

_____

_____

_____

19. Loan Origination:

_____

_____

_____

_____

_____

20. Hazard Insurance:

_____

_____

_____

_____

_____

21.   Ginnie Mae:

_____

_____

_____

_____

_____

_____

22.   Fair Credit Reporting Act:

_____

_____

_____

_____

_____

23.   Fannie Mae:

_____

_____

_____

_____

_____

_____

Self-Test Answer Keys

Name
Loan Officer Answer Key
Fundamentals
Instructor:
Score:

1. What are the two classifications within the mortgage market/
    Primary Mortgage Market

    Secondary Mortgage Market

2. What is an investing pool?

    A group of smaller investors seeking a low risk, long term investment and having
    capital available to purchase packaged loan products

3. What are the three most common employment opportunities for a loan Officer?

    Bank

    Brokerage Office

    E Commute

4. What is the purpose of a mortgage brokerage?
    To act as a liaison between the borrowers seeking mortgage funds and multiple
    funding sources.

5. What are the most common entities within the secondary mortgage market/
    Insurance Companies
    Primary Lenders with excess deposits
    Pension funds
    Individual investors

6. Which is not a common entity within the primary mortgage market?
    d.   Insurance Company

Name
Loan Officer Answer Key
Fundamentals – Ethics and Disclosure
Instructor:
Score:

1.   What is the purpose of the laws that govern the ethics and disclosures with which you handle loan processes?

   To protect the interest of the public and make the obtainment of housing and home mortgage funds a fair practice for all applicants.

2.   What is HMDA?
   The home mortgage disclosure act

3.   What is the purpose of fair housing laws?
   To prevent discrimination against any borrower in the sale, rental, financing, or other housing related transaction

4.   What other act assists in the prevention of discrimination against applicants?
   The equal credit opportunity act

5.   What items are illegal for use in evaluating applicant's qualifications?
   Race, color, religion, sex, national origin, marital status, age, source of income, handicap, and familial status

6.   What are the three common notices you might provide an applicant with regard to their credit application?
   Approval, counter-offer, or denial

7.   What is RESPA?
   Real Estate Settlement Procedures Act, which helps consumers shop for settlement services and eliminates referral fees that increase the costs of certain settlement services

8.   What is the disclosure notice requirement if a loan is transferred to a new servicer?
   15 days

9.   What is a settlement statement?
   HUD 1 is the statement that itemizes all of the closing costs payable at the closing.

10. What is TILA?
The truth-in-lending act that is part of the consumer credit protection act. The act is meant to protect and inform the consumer by requiring specific disclosures regarding the loan terms and costs.

11. When must a right to cancel be provided?
Any credit transaction that involves a security interest in a borrower's primary residence must provide the borrower with the right to rescind.

12. Explain the reason for HOEPA.
The homeowner's equity protection act is designed to protect a borrower against unfair and abusive lending tactics.

13. When will PMI be automatically cancelled in a normal risk mortgage?
When the borrower's equity position reaches 22% if the borrower is current on mortgage payments or when the borrower reaches a 22% or greater equity position and the borrower brings their mortgage obligations current.

14. When will PMI be automatically cancelled in a high-risk mortgage?
When the loan reaches a 77% LTV, or the loan reaches the half-life whichever occurs first in time.

15. What is HUD and what is their function?
Department of Housing and Urban Development that is not a direct lender but rather maintains an ongoing program to monitor the quality of HUD originated loans.

16. What is PMI?
Private Mortgage Insurance – a policy that protects the lenders who make loans to individuals without obtaining a full 20% down payment.

17. What is the annual mortgage-insurance premium?
5% of the loan amount paid at a rate of 1/12 of the overall premium monthly

18. Why have ethics and disclosure laws been created?

    D   All of the above

19. The loan Officer must:

    D   all of the above

20   Many states have created educational and licensure requirements for lending professionals.

A   True

21.   HMDA requires the reporting of

C   public loan data

22.   Information for the HMDA reports should be gathered:

C   at the initial application

23.   Fair housing laws are designed to prevent

A   discrimination in a credit related transaction

24   ECOA is

C   equal credit opportunity act

25.   ECOA addresses:

D   all of the above

26.   RESPA

D   All of the above

27.   A point is .10 percent of the loan amount

B   False

28.   The borrower has the right to cancel any credit transaction involving their home within 3 days of the funding of the transaction.

B   False

29   All borrowers must purchase flood insurance

    B.   False

30.   HUD is a direct lender

    B   False

31.   The automatic insurance premium cancellation requires that the principal balance of the loan fall below:

    A   78%

1. What is the primary reason that many loan Officers fail to obtain the information that will be needed for a pre-qualification?

    Because they are afraid to ask for information

2. What is the essential element to gaining the information you need from a borrower?
    You must ask for the information

3. Why is the initial contact with any potential borrower important?
    The initial contact sets the tone for the entire relationship with that borrower. Most people will make decisions concerning your professionalism and character within the first 30 seconds of contact.

4. Why should you request referral information of each pre-qualification?
    To assist in tracking referral source information, assessing marketing and advertising effectiveness and to provide follow-up information regarding the applicant to the referral source

5. Why do you ask if the applicant has chosen a home to purchase during the pre-qualification interview?
    This question enables you to assess the urgency of the query and determine if the borrower thus enabling you to prioritize the flow of work within your office.

    You will also be able to determine if the borrower is working with an agent thereby strengthening referral relationships.

    If the borrower has chosen a home, you will be able to use real purchase numbers to assess DTI and borrower expectations prior to the first face-to-face meeting.

6.   What is your most important product?
      The professionalism, attentiveness, and responsiveness you provide to your
      borrowers.

7.   Most loan inquiries are taken
      D   both b & c

8.   Your most valuable tool in planning a loan strategy is
      B   information

9.   The pre-approval questionnaire contains
      B   most of the information you will need for the loan application

10.   The initial contact
      A   sets the tone for your relationship with the borrower

11.   You will request a credit authorization verbally before pulling borrower credit.
      B   False

12.   You may enter common nicknames for the borrower
      B   False

13.   You must always have a co-borrower for the loan
      B   False

14.   You should complete the pre-qualification questionnaire as soon as the borrower
      locates the home they wish to purchase
      B   False

15. The most important lending product is

   B   professionalism and responsiveness

16. The pre-qualification questionnaire will provide you with

   B   information that will be noted in the explanation of credit section

1.   What does a credit report show about a borrower?
        Credit reports are an overview of a person's history of spending and payment habits.

2.   What is your primary concern when reviewing a borrower's credit report?
        Any action that had a negative or derogatory impact on a borrower's credit history.

3.   What is the score range you can expect to see on a credit report?
        450 to 850

4.   What are the three credit bureaus you will encounter?
        Beacon at Equifax
        Empirica at Transunion
        TRW/Fair Isaac at TRW

5.   What is a FICO?
        The Fair, Isaac Credit Bureau Score

6.   How is the FICO generated?
        The FICO is generated using a system of scorecards created by compiling the credit
        data from millions of consumers and then applying complex mathematical methods
        and extensive research to note credit patterns that predict probable credit
        performance.

7.   Fair, Isaac credit bureau scores do NOT use what as predictive characteristics:
        Race, color, religion, national origin, sex, marital status, age, occupation, length of
        time at present housing, or any information not contained within the credit file

8.   What do credit bureau scores provide to a lender?
     A means of rank ordering potential borrowers based on the likelihood that they would pay their obligations as agreed

9.   How can you gain information to assist you in understanding why a credit report scored the way it did?
     By reviewing the score factor reason codes included on the report

10. Credit Reports are:
     C.   An overview of a person's entire history of spending and payment

11   Credit reports are an overview of a person's entire history of spending and payment habits.
     C.   True

12. A bankruptcy can remain on a credit report for
     B.   7 years

13. Accounts to medical services that a borrower has failed to pay as agreed are
     A.   Often treated differently

14. Repeatedly requesting a borrower's credit report may
     A.   Adversely affect the credit score

15. A late payment is any payment paid past the due date even when within the grace period
     B.   False

16. Credit bureau scores are based upon
     B.   The data contained within the credit bureau

17. A credit bureau score will rank order potential borrowers based upon the number of good loans to bad loans.
     A.   True

Name
Loan Officer Answer Key
Practice – Compensating Factors and DTI
Instructor:
Score:

1.   What is a compensating factor?
      Any items that exist in the borrower's profile that may exceed the normal
      circumstances commonly encountered and reflect favorably on the borrower

2.   Why do you use compensating factors?
      To provide underwriting with a solid reason to approve a borrower at a higher level
      when that borrower falls on the edge of a credit tier or approval level

3.   Name three potential compensating factors:
      Less than 10% increase from the old rent/housing payments to the new housing
      expense.

      A decrease from the old rent/housing payments to the new housing expense

      A borrower's excellent savings ability (as shown by savings accounts, etc)

      Income that is not qualifying income

      Larger than minimum down payment

      Residual income (excess after expense) of $500 per adult and $250 per child

      Time at current residence exceeds 5 years.

      Time at current employment exceeds 5 years.

      Debt-to-income ratios below maximum guidelines as set forth for that approval level.

      Credit scores fall within a few points of next highest level.

      A perfect mortgage or rental history, as proven through the credit bureau

4.   What does a debt ratio tell you about a file?
        How much loan borrowers can afford

5.   What is a front-end ratio?
        The gross income divided by the new PITI mortgage payment

6.   Which ratio is defined as the gross income divided by the new PITI mortgage
        payment and the minimum monthly payment from all other liabilities?
        The back end ratio

7.   Name three items not commonly factored into the debt ratio:
        Utility Bills
        Car Insurance
        Health Insurance
        Cell Phone Bills

8.   What are three methods that you might employ to assist in adjusting debt ratios?
        Pay off certain items
        Lower the interest rate of the new loan
        Lower the loan amount offered to the borrower

9.   How many times do you factor each debt when calculating debt ratios?
        One time, regardless of the number of times the debt appears in the report(s).

10.   Whose income and credit history do you use when calculating debt-to-income ratio
        for married applicants?
        Both parties' income and credit history is considered, but you factor each debt only
        once even if it appears on both credit reports.

11.   Explain the premise of debt-to-income ratios.
        Debt-to-income ratio's are the amount of open debt a borrower carries weighed
        against the borrower's monthly income and in general, the higher the DTI the greater
        the potential risk of borrower default on a loan.

12. Gross income is:
Income before taxes

13. Explain the formula for factoring a potential mortgage payment.
Gross monthly income x 29% (max qualifying ratio) = Max Mortgage Payment

14. What is a compensating factor and why is it important?
A compensating factor is any item that exists in the borrower's profile that falls outside of the standard or norm and may reflect favorably on the borrower from the perspective of the underwriter.

A compensating factor may be used to overcome any item that exists in the borrower's profile that falls outside or exceeds standard guideline criteria.

15 When a borrower falls just below or on the edge of a credit tier, you may
B. Request an exception

16. The debt ratio will determine
C. How much additional debt a borrower can afford

17. Which monthly liability will not be used to calculate the debt ratio?
C. Utilities

18. The Debt-to-Income Ratio can be adjusted if
D. All of the above

19. A compensating factor would be
D. All of the above

20. A compensating factor is used to
A. Exceed normal guidelines

21. You will calculate the debt ratio using
A. Gross Income

22. The ability to borrow more money is affected by
    A. How much debt potential a borrower currently carries

23. Debt to Income is
    D. None of the above

1. Why is it important to include the amortization method planned for a loan package on the initial application?
    The amortization method dictates the monthly payment, debt load, and types of disclosures required on an application.

2. What is the appropriate entry on the application if a borrower is applying for a pre-approval with no property in mind?
    To be decided

3. Why is it important to enter information regarding the use the borrower plans to make of the property?
    Approval levels will vary depending on the occupancy status of the property.

4. What factors may alter the source of funds information entered as the loan process moves toward completion?
    Subordinate finance negotiated
    Seller assistance toward closing costs
    Sales price
    Other possible factors not yet visible

5. What action should you take if you need additional space to reference residence history, employment history, debt information or other borrower specific information that needs to be included in the application?
    You should include additional information on the last page of the application.

6. Why would you include borrower income that cannot be used for qualifying purposes on the application?
    To bring this information to the attention of the underwriter early in the process in order to set the stage for compensating factors in the event an exception is required.

7. What monthly payment amount will you enter for a revolving liability that currently has not balance?
    A standard figure is $15.00 for each revolving line the applicant has available if the balance is zero but the specific underwriting guidelines for the loan program you are planning should be consulted.

8. What is the premise behind requesting the highest loan amount that a borrower will be eligible to receive when submitting for a pre-approval that has no actual subject property?
You can easily lower the loan amount later but an increase in the loan amount requested will require the underwriting department to recalculate all numbers and issue a new approval.

9. Why should you include any information you have regarding possible subordinate financing early in the approval process?
Including the terms of a subordinate finance agreement early in the process allows the underwriter to approve or decline the terms of subordinate financing before the deal has progressed.

10. If you do not use the space provided on the continuation sheet page what action should you take?
If the space available for additional information is not used you should cross through the blank area. This crossing through assures the borrower that you will not alter or add any items to their application after their signature is affixed.

11. The method of amortization should be included on the loan application because
D. All of the above

12. You must always have the subject property address prior to completing the loan application.
B. False

13. Federal Housing Acts have differing guidelines for
D. All of the above

14. Occupancy Status will effect
A. Approval Levels

15. It is a portion of your job function to assist borrowers in determining the source of funds to be used in a transaction.
A. True

16. Non-qualifying income should be disclosed
C. Only at the request of the borrower

17. Pre-paid items are dictated by
B. underwriting guidelines

18.   Seller concession toward closing costs must appear
       D. all of the above

1. Why is an appraisal vital to the loan process?
    A borrower is responsible for repaying the loan but the property acts as collateral in the event the borrower does not fulfill their obligations.

2. What is a red flag?
    Any information that appears regarding issues that will stand in the way of the completion of the loan

3. What is URAR?
    Uniform Residential Appraisal Report

4. What is your goal when reviewing an appraisal?
    To scrutinize any item that appears to vary between documents in the file and the entries on the appraisal to determine which document contains the error and to note any item that is below the minimum requirements of the loan guideline, which you are planning for the loan file.

5. What action should you take if you discover an error in a loan document?
    You should have the person responsible for the errors address them in writing.

6. Why is it important to locate red flags early in the process?
    Because it is sometimes more effective and a faster process to request the necessary correction items or additional information immediately rather than waiting for the underwriter to generate a stipulation regarding the matter.

7. What alterations should you make to a completed appraisal if you discover an issue during your review?
    You should only request alterations arising because of an error or omission not an alteration to the opinion or decision of the appraiser.

8. What does the sales comparison valuation approach consider?
    The sales comparison approach assesses the characteristics of the subject property as compared to other similar properties sold within a given time period.

9.	The property in a loan process is as important a factor as borrower history
	A. True

10.	The appraisal will be used for
	D. All of the above

11.	URAR is an abbreviation for
	A. The Uniform Residential Appraisal Report

12.	The appraiser will note Red Flags during the appraisal process
	A. True

13.	The appraiser will assess
	D. All of the above

14.	You should never read the appraisal before underwriting
	B. False

15.	If you note a discrepancy, error or issue on the appraisal report you should
	C. Notify the appraiser of the issue

16.	Property Valuation will be determined by
	D. All of the above

Name
Loan Officer Basic Training
Answer Key
Practice – Guideline Matrix
Mentor:
Score:

1.   Why is it important to become familiar with the guidelines of the various loan products available through your branch?
The more familiar with loan guidelines you become the more capable you will be at moving the loan package through the loan process and to a successful closing. Familiarity allows you to locate and address any red flag issues that may be apparent before an issue inhibits the closing of the loan.

2.   What is a product matrix?
A snapshot of the minimum requirements needed to place a loan in a particular program and approval level.

3.   What is the first step in grading a package for loan placement?
Rate the credit report scoring key elements against the product matrix levels.

4.   What factor may alter the pricing you initially plan for a loan placement?
The debt ratio may change after you price the loan because of interest rate and subsequent monthly payment. If this ratio becomes excessive, you may need to re-price the loan.

5.   What are some steps you might take if the new loan causes the borrower to exceed the ratio limitations set by the loan guidelines?
Obtain an exception to the ratio limitations with compensating factors.

Reduce the maximum sales price/loan amount the borrower may obtain.

Reduce the points wrapped in the interest rate and allow the borrower to make payment for the services of your office on the front end.

Pay off consumer debt in an attempt to reduce overall debt load.

Obtain seller assistance toward closing costs or additional borrower funds to buy down the interest rate to a level that generates a payment that fits within the borrower debt-ratio guidelines.

Search for a different program that allows the borrower to approve at the levels needed to close the loan under the present circumstances.

6.   You must place each loan carefully because there are a limited number of loan products to choose from

   B. False

7.   A product matrix is

   B. A snapshot of minimum requirements

8.   A product matrix will allow you to assess a loans suitability for your borrower.

   A. True

9.   You will begin grading using

   C. The credit-scoring key

10. You will need to compare

   B. All decisioning factors

11. You should begin grading

   B. At the highest approval tier

12. You may exceed an approval level by

   C. Supplying adequate compensating factors

13. If the housing expense exceeds the loan criteria, you must

   B. Suggest alternative options to the borrower

1. What is a pricing restriction?
   An internal limitation or requirement and applicable laws regarding loan pricing.

2. What is the second step in loan pricing?
   Review the minimum qualifying guidelines included on the rate sheet to confirm that your borrower meets the current criteria.

3. What three items must you determine prior to beginning the actual pricing?
   Preferred loan terms
   The LTV required
   Pricing including office payment

4. Who is the best candidate for a fixed rate program?
   Perpetual high-risk borrower
   Long-term purchaser
   Cautious borrower

5. What is a prepayment penalty?
   A monetary penalty which is assessed for the early payoff of a loan containing a prepay clause.

6. What common pre-pay terms do most lenders offer?
   0, 2, 3, and 5-year penalties

7. What benefit does the pre-payment penalty offer to a lender?
   Security that the borrower will retain the loan for a certain period thereby securing the expected interest payments for the lender or that if the borrower pays the loan off early the interest loss to the lender will be offset by the penalty.

8. What is the primary benefit to the use of a pre-pay penalty for the borrower?
    Lenders will often offer a reduction of the initial interest rate in exchange for the pre-payment clause because of the added longevity of loans on the books.

9. What does it mean to price at PAR?
    There are no points included in the interest rate and you must obtain payment for the branch as points charged on the good faith estimate and HUD Settlement Statement.

10. When do you use the Margin?
    When you use an ARM option in the loan, you will note the margin that refers to the rate of adjustment that may occur

11. When pricing a loan you should use
    B. The most current rate sheet

12. Pricing restrictions may occur as a result of
    D. All of the above

13. All rate sheets will include qualifying information for you to review
    B. False

14. You will determine the interest rate offered using
    D. All of the above

15. The pre-payment requirements may
    D. All of the above

Name
Loan Officer Answer Key
Fundamentals - Documentation
Instructor:
Score:

1.   Why is it important to document each loan package you submit?
      Without proper documentation, the underwriter cannot make a valid decision on the
      loan package and will request additional items or stipulations prior to issuing an
      approval or conditional approval.

2.   Why should you note any missing information on the loan cover letter that you
      submit with the package?
      To assure the underwriter that you are aware of the lacking information and are
      working to obtain all necessary documentation

3.   Why should you include compensating factor information at the time of the initial
      submittal even when an exception request is not expected?
      To set a positive tone for the loan package

      To bring the compensating factors to the attention of the underwriter before they
      initially review the borrower profile

      To set the stage if something occurs later in the process that requires a positive
      decision or exception from the underwriter

4.   Why should you include information regarding the approval and transaction specifics
      you are requesting as part of your loan cover sheet?
      This inclusion allows the underwriter to review the material and is a courtesy action
      that will smooth the underwriter's workload.

5.   What is the purpose of a stipulation list?
      To allow the underwriter to request information required for loan decision, closing or
      secondary market sale and to provide clarification information regarding any file item
      that is unclear to the underwriter.

6.   What are the three common written decisions you will see from underwriting?

      Approved   Everything contained within the file meets the guidelines for final
      approval
      Conditional   Additional documentation will be needed to ensure final loan approval
      Denied   Aspects of the file do not conform to the guidelines

7. What is an affinity provider?
   Any individual who must complete their tasks in a timely, professional manner in order for you to accomplish your goal of closing the loan

8. Who is ultimately responsible for the smooth process and timely closing of the loan?
   The loan officer

9. How can you avoid loan process delays?
   By maintaining an organized flow process, using an adequate loan process follow-up and affinity service provider reminder-system.

10. How can you foster positive relationships with affinity service providers?
    By treating these providers in a respectful, friendly, and considerate manner to foster positive relationships, build rapport and create an overall good relationship.

11. Why must you request income documentation from each borrower?
    All lenders require that a borrower have sufficient and adequate income to cover the repayment of the mortgage. The stability and probability of continuance must be established.

12. What does the mortgage or rental history tell the loan underwriter?
    The probability that the borrower will repay their new mortgage in a timely manner

13. What is a VOM?
    Verification of Mortgage

14. What is a CLTV?
    Combined Loan to Value

15. Explain the general rule regarding credit risk and borrower investment.
    Generally, the higher the credit risks the higher percentage of funds the borrower must invest.

16. Why should you request all borrower documentation at the beginning of the loan process?
    To ensure you are able to verify information, structure the loan package correctly, and request supporting information in an efficient manner.

17. Overtime and bonus income may be used to qualify a borrower providing there is:

    A two-year history

18. What type of rental income is an acceptable source of income?

    D   Income from an investment property received under a lease

19. What percentage of business must a borrower own to be considered self-employed?

    A   25%

20. A borrower may choose to use alimony, child support, or separate maintenance if they provide what documentation?

    D   Both A & B

21. Mortgage or rental history is often used to project the probability of a borrower repaying their new mortgage in a timely manner.

    A   True

22. If the mortgage or rental history is not included in the credit report, which of the following is an acceptable replacement?

    D   Both A & C

23. Bank statement as income documentation programs are typically not penalized with a higher interest or down payment requirement because the statements are considered full documentation.

    B   False

24. An outright gift of money toward a purchase of a home is typically acceptable if it is a gift from:

    A   A charitable organization

25. The loan officer is the liaison between

    B   the borrower and underwriting

26. Each time you submit a stipulation the underwriter will

   A   review the entire loan file

27. If you must repeatedly return to the borrower for additional documentation, you will gain

   B   a poor reputation

28. The underwriting summary is a form of

   A   checklist of inclusions

29. When requesting an appraisal you should note

   B   the method of billing and payment

30. The most important product a Loan Officer has available is

   C   customer service skills

31. The first act you will take on a loan package is to

   C   complete the pre-qualification

32. You should revise the good faith estimate

   C   upon receipt of the sales agreement

33. The borrower should be informed of the final loan specifics

   A   before the closing

34. The loan officer should take gifts to the closing

   B   False

35. The underwriter will review all aspects of the file including:

   D   All of the above

36. The underwriter will review the file and issue an

    D   Any of the above

37. Prior to closing documents must be provided to the underwriter before the loan documents can be requested.

    B   False

38. The processing stage is a stage where

    D   all of the above

39. A verification of deposit is a form sent

    B   To the bank to verify the average bank account balance of the borrower

40. The funding is when

    B   the monies borrowed are wired or sent to the closing agent

41. Delays in the loan process can be avoided by

    D   all of the above

42. Many loan Officers forget to create

    C   positive service relationships

43. An affinity service provider includes any individual who must accomplish tasks in a timely and professional manner in order for you to accomplish your goal of closed loans.

    A   True

44. You should treat your affinity service providers

    D   All of the above

KEY TERMS AND DEFINITIONS

1.   Closing costs:

Expenses incurred by buyers and sellers in transferring ownership of a property. Closing costs normally include an origination fee, an attorney's fee, taxes, escrow payments, and charges for title insurance. Lenders or Real Estate Agents provide estimates of closing costs to prospective homebuyers

2.   VA Mortgage:
A loan backed by the Veterans Administration. It requires very low or no down payments and has less stringent requirements for qualification. Members of the US armed forces are eligible for the loans under certain qualifying conditions

3.   Amortization Schedule:
A timetable for the gradual repayment of a mortgage loan. An amortization schedule indicates the amount of each payment applied to interest and principal, and the remaining balance after each payment is made

4.   Closing:
The meeting at which the sale of a property is finalized. The buyer signs the lender agreement for the mortgage and pays' closing costs and escrow amounts. The buyer and seller sign documents to transfer the ownership of the property. Also known as the settlement

5.   Title search:
A check of title records to ensure that the seller is the legal owner of a property and that there are no liens or other claims against the property

6.   Disbursement:
The release of funds held in an escrow account

7.   Credit report:
A report on a person's credit history prepared by a credit bureau and used by a lender in determining a loan applicant's record for paying debts in a timely manner

8.   Acceleration Clause:
The section of a mortgage document that allows the lender to speed up the   payment date in the event of default, making the entire principal amount due

9. Loan-to-value (LTV) Ratio:
   The ratio of a mortgage loan amount to the property's appraised value or selling price, whichever is less. For example, if a home is sold for $100,000 and the mortgage amount is $80,000 the LTV is 80%

10. Housing Expense:
    The percentage of gross monthly income that goes toward paying a Ratio mortgage or rent on a home

11. Pre-approval:
    This process goes a step further than pre-qualification. It means the lender has contacted the borrower's employer, bank, and other places to verify all claims of earnings and assets. In return, the borrower receives a letter stating the lender is willing to grant a mortgage for a specific amount within a limited period with the stipulation that there are no material changes to the borrower's situation

12. Good Faith Estimate:
    A written estimate of closing costs that the lender must provide to   prospective homebuyers within three days of submitting a mortgage loan application

13. Freddie Mac:
    Nickname for Federal Home Loan Mortgage Corp. A financial corporation chartered by the federal government to buy pools of mortgages from lenders and sell securities backed by these mortgages

14. Debt-to-Income Ratio:
    The percentage of a person's monthly earnings used to pay off all debt obligations. Lenders consider two ratios, constructed in slightly different ways. The first called the front-end ratio, the ratio of the monthly housing expenses – including principal, interest, property taxes, and insurance, (PITI) is compared to the borrower's gross, pretax monthly income. In the back-end ratio, a borrower's other debts such as auto loans and credit cards are figured in. Lenders usually consider both and set an acceptable ratio. Some lenders and some lending qualifying agencies only consider the back-end ratio

15. Comparables:
    Refers to "comparable properties" which are used for comparative purposes in the appraisal process. Comps are recently sold properties that are similar in size, location, and amenities to the home for sale. Comps help an appraiser determine the fair market value of a property

16. RESPA:
    Real Estate Settlement Procedures Act. A consumer protection law that requires lenders to give homebuyers advance notice of closing costs, which are payable at the closing or settlement meeting

17. Pre-qualification:
An early evaluation by a lender of a potential homebuyer's credit report, plus earnings, savings, and debt information   The homebuyer gets a non-binding estimate of the mortgage amount the borrower would qualify for, or how much house the borrower can afford. Buyers who pre-qualify can go a step further and seek a pre-approval

18. PITI Reserves:
A cash amount that a homebuyer must have on hand after making a down payment and paying all closing costs. The reserves required by a lender must equal the amount a buyer would pay for PITI for a specific number of months

19. Loan Origination:
The process by which a mortgage lender obtains a mortgage secured by real property. An origination fee is charged by the lender to process all forms involved in obtaining a mortgage

20. Hazard Insurance:
Insurance coverage that compensates for physical damage to property from natural disasters such as fire and other hazards Depending on where a piece of property is located, lenders may also require flood insurance or policies covering windstorms (hurricanes) or earthquakes

21. Ginnie Mae:
Nickname for the Government National Mortgage Association

22. Fair Credit Reporting Act:
A consumer protection law that regulates the disclosure of consumer credit reports by credit reporting agencies and establishes procedures for correcting mistakes on a person's credit record

23. Fannie Mae:
Nickname for Federal National Mortgage Association. It is a government-chartered non-bank financial services company and the nation's largest source of financing for home mortgages. It was started to make sure mortgage money is available in all areas of the country

Creative Loan Structure
Mortgage Math

Creative Loan Structure

There will be many times when your strength at creatively structuring a loan package will gain you closings your competition cannot achieve. This method of creative loan structuring is what sets a well-trained and certified Loan Officer well above the basic marketing originator or the paper-pushing officer.

Creative structuring begins when you determine your borrower's exact financial situation and compare it to their exact wants and needs.

A borrower with no cash and a Credit Level D approval rating who wishes to purchase a $100,000 home will create one type of structure difficulty. A borrower who owns a $100,000 home and has a DTI of 55% before you begin the process and an excellent credit history creates another type of difficulty.

You will note that as you move you through the loan structure it is often necessary to work backwards. Taking the dollar value needs and filling in the sources of funding, concession, required property value, etc. to suit that particular package rather than following an in the box style scenario.

To rise to the top of your new profession you must maintain a flexible approach and an open mind when reviewing each loan package that crosses your desk. The key point in creatively structuring is to keep all the options of funds to close a package available in your head. Relying only on the borrowers own funds and the loan amount to close loans simply will not work. The loan amount, subordinate financing, seller concession toward closing costs, gift funds, sale of personal property, increased appraised value, even gifts of equity between family members are all source of funds options. Keep an open mind and make sure you ask your borrower questions and creative structuring will come easily.

Below is a breakdown of funds to close a purchase mortgage. Each package you look at must balance financially before it can be considered a "real deal".

#1 REFINANCE

Borrowers who own their home but need to refinance to do some repairs and to pay off existing debt loan qualify for a LTV of 80%.

Appraised Value	$75,000
X LTV %	x 80%
= Loan Amount	$60,000
Loan Amount	$60,000
- Existing Mortgage Pay off	-$37,753
= Available Cash	$22,247

Less any Debt to Pay Off	-$ 5,487	Cash Needed for Repairs
	-$ 1,742	Collection Debt
	-$ 9,487	Credit Cards/Personal Loans
Cash Available for Closing Costs	$ 5,531	

Note that you are building this in order. You are taking the appraised value and structuring the loan package around that figure. You may also structure the package backwards. You may wish to do this when a borrower first interviews with you to get an estimate of the loan amount and appraised value needed for the package. To structure in a reverse order you simply take all the figures in reverse.

Closing Costs	$ 5,531
+ Cash Needed for Repairs	$ 5,487
+ Funds to pay off Collection/Debt	$ 1,742
+ Funds to pay off Consumer Debt	$ 9,487
+ Existing Mortgage Pay Off	$37,753
Total Funds Needed	$60,000
Divided by LTV Approval	.80%
Appraised Value Needed	$75,000

#2 PURCHASE

Borrowers with A- Credit want to purchase a home listed for $92,000.
The credit scenario does not qualify them for a Government Loan.
They have $4,800 of their own funds available toward the purchase.
The current debt loan is 21% and with the house, the debt load is 40.67%.
The maximum DTI allowed under their program guideline is 55%.
The loan approval is for a 90% LTV with a 95% CLTV maximum.
Seller Concession is limited to 6%.

Structure

The first item to determine is the amount of cash needed to close the loan. This figure will
include the sales price of the property plus all closing costs.

Sales Price	$92,000
+ Closing Costs	$ 4,279
= Cash needed	$96,279

The second item to determine is the loan amount. That is the sales price multiplied by the
LTV approval.

Sales Price	$92,000
X LTV	.90%
Loan Amount	$82,800

Now you need to determine the source of all funds to close the loan. Begin by taking the
total for all cash needed for closing the loan and deducting the amounts you have available.
The result is the amount of funds you are short for closing.

Cash Needed	$96,279
-Loan Amount	$82,800
-Borrowers Funds	$ 4,800
Additional Funds	$ 8,679

You must find these funds in order for the loan to close.

The first option to look at is typically – will the sellers pay a portion of the closing costs from
the loan proceeds. At times, the sellers will agree to this added request if the borrowers are
willing to raise the purchase price. This option is typically easier to negotiate if the Sales

Agreement has not yet been finalized. If the sales agreement has been finalized, Underwriting will not usually allow a "bump" or increase in the sales price. Check the loan guidelines to determine the maximum amount of seller concession allowed under the borrower's loan program. Remember – you work for the borrower in this transaction! In this scenario, you are allowed up to 6% of the sales price to be contributed by the seller towards the borrower's non-recurring closing costs. 6% of the sales price is $5,520. The closing costs in this scenario only total $4279. Although the maximum allowed is $5,520, the sellers will not be able to contribute the maximum amount but only the amount of actual costs. If you have not disclosed closing costs, this is an excellent opportunity to add more fees for you into the overall closing figures.

The second option to look at is do the borrowers have any additional funds available. Some borrowers may have a retirement or investment account that may be cashed out from which funds may be borrowed. If borrowers, keep in mind that the re-payment figure must meet DTI guidelines. Some borrowers may have personal property available for sale. If personal property is sold, you must properly document the sale of the property including proving ownership of the property in the first place and fair market value of the property. Gift funds from a family member, agency designed for the purpose of helping people purchase homes or the borrowers employer may also be used providing a letter is signed stating that the funds will not be repaid.

The last option available is secondary financing. In this case, the borrowers are allowed up to 5% of the sales price in the form of a loan. Secondary financing may come from the seller. This financing must be negotiated on the Sales Agreement and must be secured against the property being purchased in the form of a second mortgage. Secondary financing may also be secured through another financing company. Any secondary financing must be by contract and the monthly repayment must meet the borrowers DTI Ratio guidelines.

In this scenario, we will use a combination of those items:

$ 8,679	Additional Funds Needed to Close
-$ 4,279	Seller Concession toward Non-Recurring Closing Costs
-$ 1,200	Sale of borrower property sourced with Bill of Sale
-$ 3,200	Second Mortgage held by Seller with 0% interest and monthly payment of $55.00 per month for 57 months with one payment of $65.00
$ 0	Funds unaccounted for toward cost of property.

The ability to creatively source funds to close will allow you a greater ability to close loans than your less creative counterparts. Many Originators quit after the initial inquiry upon discovering the limited resources of cash on hand available to the borrower. The act of digging deeper and using your creativity allows you to present options that your borrowers may not have considered toward sourcing funds.

DEBT-TO-INCOME RATIO EXCERCISES

To calculate a borrower's debt to income take the total monthly debt load and divide it by the total monthly income. For example:

A borrower who earns $2800.00 monthly and has installment debt of $750.00 monthly has a debt-to-income ratio of 26.78%.

D   I   R

750 / 2800 = 26.78%

1. Income$6200
    Debt $1900

    _____
    Ratio   %

2. Income$3000
    Debt $1350

    _____
    Ratio   %

3. Income$3750
    Debt $ 970

    _____
    Ratio   %

4. Income$1600
    Debt $ 340

    _____
    Ratio   %

5. Income$2000
    Debt $ 420

    _____
    Ratio   %

6. Income$2480
    Debt $ 920

    _____
    Ratio   %

7. Income$4200
    Debt $1850

    _____
    Ratio   %

8. Income$4800
    Debt $2175

    _____
    Ratio   %

9. Income$5100
    Debt $1950

    _____
    Ratio   %

10. Income$5500
    Debt $1775

    _____
    Ratio   %

11. Income$5750
    Debt $1900

    _____
    Ratio   %

12. Income$3425
    Debt $1350

    _____
    Ratio   %

13. Income$4387
    Debt $1218

    _____

14. Income$2330
    Debt $ 961

    _____

CALCULATING LOAN-TO-VALUE

When calculating loan to value, assuming the Value and the LTV Percentage are given the formula is Value multiplied by percentage.

Assume a house with a value (sales price) of $112,000 with a LTV of 95% would have a loan amount of $106,400.

	Sales Price	x LTV Percentage	= Loan Amount
	$112,000	x .95	= $106,400

1. Sales Price $99,000
    LTV   85%

    _____
    Loan $

2. Sales Price $110,000
    LTV   90%

    _____
    Loan $

3. Sales Price $144,900
    LTV   95%

    _____
    Loan $

4. Sales Price $75,000
    LTV   80%

    _____
    Loan $

5. Sales Price $69,900
    LTV   70%

    _____
    Loan $

6. Sales Price $104,900
    LTV   75%

    _____
    Loan $

CALCULATING COMBINED LOAN TO VALUE

When a Combined Loan-to-Value is offered, you will calculate the secondary financing figure using the same formula above.

Sales Price   x CLTV Percentage = Subordinate/Secondary Financing Loan Amount
$112,000   x .05   = $5600 maximum second mortgage

1.   Sales Price $99,000

      LTV 85% CLTV 95%

      _____
      Loan $

2.   Sales Price $110,000

      LTV 90%   CLTV 95%

      _____
      Loan $

3.   Sales Price $144,900
      LTV 90% CLTV 95%

      _____
      Loan $

4.   Sales Price $75,000
      LTV 80%   CLTV 90%

      _____
      Loan $

5.   Sales Price $69,900
      LTV 70% CLTV 80%

      _____
      Loan $

6.   Sales Price $104,900
      LTV 75% CLTV 85%

      _____
      Loan $

Any funds toward the purchase price not included in LTV or CLTV will be required as cash invested on the part of the borrower. Funds for closing costs may be acquired through other means.

SELLER CONCESSION

When calculating seller concession toward borrower's non-recurring closing costs you will want to use the SALES PRICE of the property as your base number. The seller concession figure is negotiated in the sales agreement and can be a fixed dollar amount or it may be a percentage. For these exercises, assume the seller is willing to grant 6% of the sales price toward borrower's non-recurring closing costs.

Sales Price	x Concession Percentage	= Dollar Concession Amount
$112,000	x 6%	= $6720

1.   Sales Price $99,000

2.   Sales Price $110,000

3.   Sales Price $144,900

4.   Sales Price $75,000

5.   Sales Price $69,900

6.   Sales Price $104,900

7.   Sales Price $49,500

8.   Sales Price $219,900

9.   Sales Price $53,350

10.   Sales Price $189,000

SELLER CONCESSION

For additional exercise in calculating maximum seller concession, you can calculate using a maximum seller concession toward buyer's non-recurring closing costs of 3% of the sales price. (6% and 3% are the most commonly allowed maximum seller concessions under most underwriting guidelines.)

Sales Price	**x Concession Percentage**	**= Dollar Concession Amount**
$112,000	**x 3%**	**= $3360**

1. Sales Price $99,000

2. Sales Price $110,000

3. Sales Price $144,900

4. Sales Price $75,000

5. Sales Price $69,900

6. Sales Price $104,900

7. Sales Price $49,500

8. Sales Price $219,900

9. Sales Price $53,350

10. Sales Price $189,000

MAXIMUM HOUSING EXPENSE (PITI)

It is important to be able to calculate the maximum monthly housing expense (PITI – Principal, Interest, Taxes, and Insurance) your borrower could afford under any loan program approval. This allows you to set borrowers and Agents expectations as to the cost range of properties that the borrowers should be shopping.

Begin with the maximum DTI as per the approval level. Subtract the borrowers current DTI (excluding any housing expense from the ratio). The total is the percentage of income available to spend on PITI. This percentage should be multiplied by the borrower's total monthly income to achieve a maximum dollar amount that may be spent toward PITI.

The formula for calculating Maximum PITI payments is as follows:

Maximum DTI %	**– Current DTI %**	**= % Income Available for Housing Costs**
41%	- 22%	= 19%

Monthly Income	**X % of Income Available for PITI**	**= Maximum Mthly PITI**
$3200	X 19%	= $608 maximum PITI

For the following problems, assume a maximum DTI of 45%

1. Current DTI   29%
   Income $3750

2. Current DTI 18%
   Income $2100

3. Current DTI   22%
   Income $2880

4. Current DTI 31%
   Income $4195

5. Current DTI   24%
   Income $2655

6. Current DTI 12%
   Income $3875

7. Current DTI   19%
   Income $3150

8. Current DTI 26%
   Income $1775

9. Current DTI   14%
   Income $1980

10. Current DTI 36%
    Income $3650

LENDING MATH ANSWER KEY

DTI RATIOS
1. 31%
2. 45%
3. 26%
4. 21%
5. 21%
6. 37%
7. 44%
8. 45%
9. 38%
10. 32%
11. 33%
12. 39%

LTV
1. $ 84,150
2. $ 99,000
3. $137,655
4. $ 60,000
5. $ 48,930
6. $ 78,675

CLTV
1. $ 9,900
2. $ 5,500
3. $ 7,245
4. $ 7,500
5. $ 6,990
6. $10,490

SELLER CONCESSION 6%
1. $ 5,940
2. $ 6,600
3. $ 8,694
4. $ 4,500
5. $ 4,194
6. $ 6,294
7. $ 2,970
8. $13,194
9. $ 3,201
10. $11,340

SELLER CONCESSION 3%
1. $2,970.00
2. $3,300.00
3. $4,347.00
4. $2,250.00
5. $2,097.00
6. $3,147.00
7. $1,485.00
8. $6,597.00
9. $1,600.50
10. $5,670.00

MAXIMUM MONTHLY PITI PAYMENT

	Ratio for PITI	$ Value for PITI
1.	12%	$ 450.00
2.	23%	$ 483.00
3.	19%	$ 547.20
4.	10%	$ 419.50
5.	17%	$ 451.35
6.	29%	$1123.75
7.	22%	$ 693.00
8.	15%	$ 266.25
9.	27%	$ 534.60
10.	5%	$ 182.50

www.ingramcontent.com/pod-product-compliance
Lightning Source LLC
Chambersburg PA
CBHW082355270326
41935CB00013B/1635